THE HEART OF PRAYER

The Heart of Prayer

What Jesus Teaches Us

Jerram Barrs

P U B L I S H I N G
P.O. BOX 817 • PHILLIPSBURG • NEW JERSEY 08865-0817

Library of Congress Cataloging-in-Publication Data

Barrs, Jerram.
The heart of prayer : what Jesus teaches us / Jerram Barrs.
    p. cm.
Includes bibliographical references.
ISBN 978-1-59638-103-2 (pbk.)
1. Lord's prayer. 2. Prayer—Biblical teaching. 3. Prayer—Christianity. 4. Jesus Christ—Teachings. I. Title.
BV230.B367 2008
248.3'2—dc22
                                        2007043466

To my three sons: Peter, Paul, and Philip, and to my seven (so far) grandchildren: James, Ethan, Harry, Eliana, Isaac, Owen, and Jesse. My sons, when you were little children, and you, my grandchildren, have taught me much of what I know about prayer by your example. May your heavenly Father shower his love into your hearts, both now and for all eternity to come.

CONTENTS

INTRODUCTION

As will become clear to you when you read this book, I have never thought of myself as an expert, either in the practice of prayer, or in reflection on the theology of prayer. "Why, then," you may ask very reasonably, "have you written a book on prayer?" There is a simple answer to this which I hope and pray will satisfy, you, the reader. I have found Jesus' teaching on prayer, and the example of his prayers, so personally encouraging to me that, like a little child who discovers something especially interesting or beautiful, I want to share with others what I have been learning from the Lord.

My primary thanks for anything helpful in this book must go to the Lord Jesus himself. The mistakes and anything unhelpful are my responsibility only, and I ask him for his forgiveness for these errors.

In addition to thanking the Lord, I also wish to thank my sons and grandchildren for all they have taught me about prayer. Especially in prayer it seems to me that the Scripture is fulfilled which says: "A little child shall lead them" (Isa. 11:6), and that Jesus' words are particularly applicable when he prays, "I thank you, Father, Lord of heaven and earth, that you have hidden these things from the wise and understanding and revealed them to little children; yes, Father, for such was your gracious will" (Luke 10:21). The honesty,

9

directness, and simplicity of the prayers of little children catch much of the spirit of Jesus' teaching on prayer. As adults we are too aware of what others may be thinking about our prayers and of the impression we might be making on the Lord and on those around us. Consequently we lose very easily the heart of prayer, the heart that a child grasps so readily.

My thanks are due to Edith Schaeffer, whose teaching on prayer was deeply helpful, and to my colleagues on the faculty at Covenant Theological Seminary in St. Louis, whose teaching, example, and friendship is a daily joy to me.

I also wish to thank my dear wife, Vicki, whose love and encouragement are my constant companion, help, comfort, and support. Without her this book and all my teaching would simply never have happened.

Thanks also are due to the enthusiasm and help of Marvin Padgett, Eric Anest, and the rest of the editorial team at P&R Publishing.

I

LORD, TEACH US TO PRAY

Luke 11:1–4

A PERSONAL CONFESSION

I think all Christian believers who are honest with themselves and with each other will acknowledge that we are not very spiritual people, that we do not find prayer easy, and that our prayer life is not strong. And yet many of us have read books or heard sermons and talks that claim to teach us how to have a great prayer life, or how we might become prayer warriors. Some teachers even claim that their methods and approaches to prayer will guarantee spiritual experience and rich blessing from God. Some of their books become extraordinarily popular—examples are unnecessary, since everyone is familiar with them. If we pay attention to the particular teacher's approach, we are promised that such obedience will ensure our steady growth in a deep devotional life, or that God will certainly do amazing things for us—that he will "enlarge our territory" and give us answers of health, prosperity, or some other

11

great blessing. Sometimes when I hear such messages on prayer and the spiritual life, or when I read these kinds of books about prayer, I find that I go away feeling worthless and hopeless because my personal history of devotion and my practice of prayer looks very inadequate compared with what I hear and read.

Because of this sense of poverty in my prayer life, I have shied away from teaching on the subject of prayer for most of my years in ministry, first as a pastor and then as a seminary professor. What could I share when I myself was such a poor example? Some time ago, however, the dean of students at Covenant Theological Seminary, where I teach, asked me to give a talk on prayer at one of our regular days of prayer and fasting. So I thought, "Well, I had better try to come up with something." Over the past few years I had been doing a series of studies on Jesus the Greatest Evangelist, and I had found his teaching and example on this subject to be so helpful and freeing that I thought to myself: "Why not just look at what Jesus teaches about prayer? Maybe I will find the same help and freedom in Jesus' teaching on prayer that I have discovered in his teaching on evangelism."

That was exactly what I did find. As I began to look at Jesus' teaching on prayer, I found what he has to say to be the clearest, the most upbuilding, and the most healing thoughts on this subject that I had ever read. I did not have the response of feeling inadequate and worthless when I studied the message of the Lord himself. What is remarkable about this to me is that the Lord knows full well how inadequate and weak my prayer life is, and he sees my cold heart and lack of zeal; yet I find that his words on prayer are a solace and support to me, rather than a condemnation and rebuke.

So my desire in this book is to seek to encourage others with the encouragement and comfort that I myself have received from the Lord's teaching on prayer, and also from his own practice of prayer. We will begin at the beginning—with the prayer that Christians term "the Lord's Prayer."

> Now Jesus was praying in a certain place, and when he finished, one of his disciples said to him, "Lord, teach us to pray, as John taught his disciples." And he said to them, "When you pray, say:
>
>> "Father, hallowed be your name.
>>
>> Your kingdom come.
>>
>> Give us each day our daily bread,
>>
>> and forgive us our sins,
>>
>>> for we ourselves forgive everyone who is indebted to us.
>>
>> And lead us not into temptation." (Luke 11:1–4)

According to the Gospel records, Jesus taught the Lord's Prayer on two occasions—one in the Sermon on the Mount, the other in Luke chapter 11. In Matthew's gospel, the context in which Jesus teaches the Lord's Prayer is his urging those who believe in him to pray privately and not just publicly. We will look at his words on that occasion later in this book. In Luke's gospel, the setting in which we find the Lord's Prayer is quite different. The disciples see Jesus praying, and when he has finished they ask him for help: "Lord, teach us to pray, as John taught his disciples" (Luke 11:1). Why did they ask? Presumably because they did not know how to pray, or they felt that their prayers were somewhat inadequate. Perhaps their prayer life, like mine, did not amount to much! Whatever the precise reason (and we can ask them one day), they knew they needed help with their prayers.

Why did they need help? Why did they need to be taught how to pray? These are Jesus' disciples, the apostles he had chosen to be with him and to hear his teaching every day, the ones he was training to be the leaders and founders of the church all through this age. But they, of course, were just like you and me. And they needed help with their prayers, just like you and I. First, we are sinners who do nothing as we should, and so we fall short in prayer just as we do in every other area of Christian faith and life. We know that the greatest commandments are that we are to love the Lord with heart and soul and mind and strength, and to love our neighbors as ourselves. But none of us keep these commandments well. So we don't "do prayer" well, for we do not love God well, nor do we love our neighbors well.

But it seems that there is an additional problem with prayer: we do not see God face to face, for ever since the fall God has been hidden from us, and so we sense a barrier. Because we don't see the Lord, all sorts of questions come into our minds about prayer. We struggle to find time to pray; we doubt whether our prayers are "getting through" to our heavenly Father; we are uncertain about how to evaluate the reality of our prayers; we wonder whether we are praying long enough or with the right amount of fervor; we ask ourselves whether our poor motivation and the sins that beset us prevent our prayers from being heard. We could all add other anxieties and worries about our prayers to this brief list.

Be comforted, for this understanding of the problems we face with prayer is a good place to begin. It seems that the disciples were in a similar place. It is encouraging to know that the apostles clearly found prayer difficult, just as we do. Thankfully, they had the common sense, and more importantly the humility, to come to Jesus and to ask him to teach them how to pray.

For all of us, this is the beginning of learning—that is, being honest and humble enough to acknowledge that we do not do well at living the Christian life. Jesus begins the Sermon on the Mount with the words, "Blessed are the poor in spirit" (Matt. 5:3). Later on in his ministry, he says to the Pharisees, "If you were blind, you would have no guilt; but now that you say, 'We see,' your guilt remains" (John 9:41). Will we agree with Jesus that we are poor in spirit? Will we say to him: "Lord, I am blind; help me to see"? Can we move beyond having to pretend to God, to ourselves, and to others that we are deeply spiritual; that we are good at praying; that we know how to live a good Christian life; and that we love God well and love our neighbor well? Will we rather be open and humble, and will we freely acknowledge to the Lord, to ourselves, and to others that we are blind and poor and naked? It is liberating to do this, and it prepares us to be ready to learn from the Lord. So are we ready?

THE LORD'S ANSWER

And he said to them, "When you pray, say:

> "Father, hallowed be your name.
>   Your kingdom come.
>   Give us each day our daily bread,
>   and forgive us our sins,
>   for we ourselves forgive everyone who is indebted to us.
>   And lead us not into temptation." (Luke 11:2–4)

15

In reply to their request, Jesus teaches his disciples the Lord's Prayer. All through the centuries, this prayer has been regarded by the church both as a prayer for believers to pray and as a pattern for Christian prayer, a model for all our praying, whether public or private. What do we discover when we look at this model prayer?

A SHORT PRAYER

We notice first that the Lord's Prayer is a short prayer. If we time ourselves when we repeat the words that Jesus teaches us in Luke chapter 11, we will discover that it takes about fifteen seconds to say the Lord's Prayer. On the other occasion when Jesus teaches this prayer, he reminds us that God does not hear us better when we pray long prayers (Matt. 6:7). Pagans, says Jesus, pray long prayers because they think that doing so will "make God listen better." Jesus assures us that this is not the case. A prayer does not have to be long to be "spiritual." It does not have to be long for God to hear it favorably. A prayer is just as powerful, just as effective, just as pleasing to the Lord if it is a short prayer.

Jesus gives another clear example of this principle in a story he tells about the prayers of a Pharisee and a tax collector (Luke 18:9–14). Jesus represents the tax collector's prayer as very brief: "God, be merciful to me, a sinner!" (v. 13). This prayer takes just a couple of seconds, yet Jesus tells us that this man went home justified. His brief cry is a prayer that God delights to answer. Or we might think of Jesus' prayer in the garden of Gethsemane: "My Father, if it be possible, let this cup pass from me; nevertheless, not as I will, but as you will" (Matt. 26:39); or consider his prayers from the cross: "My God, my God, why have you forsaken me?" (Mark 15:34); "Father, forgive them, for they know not what they do" (Luke 23:34); and "Father, into your hands I commit my spirit!" (Luke 23:46).

God the Father was clearly pleased with these brief prayers of his Son—the Son who had dwelt close to his heart through all eternity. In just the same way, our prayers do not have to be long for God to be pleased to hear them. In fact, if our prayers are long, we might need to ask ourselves, "Why am I praying a long prayer?"

If our answer to this question is that we feel that the length of time we pray will make God more likely to listen to us, then we are wrong in a truly deep way. God hears us because of his love for us in Christ, not because we pray prayers that someone else may regard as "spiritual" because of their length. Jesus assures us that his Father is satisfied with a prayer that lasts only half a minute, or even a fleeting instant. If we answer that it is a good spiritual discipline for us to spend a good long time at our prayers, we need to ask ourselves the question: "What is prayer? Is prayer about disciplining myself to pray long prayers, or is it about talking to the Lord?" We will come back to this question later.

We may want to respond: "Aren't prayers occasionally very long? Isn't it true that some of the prayers recorded in the Bible would take a much greater time to pray than the Lord's Prayer?" We can think about some biblical examples—for instance, if we read aloud the prayer of confession that Daniel prays (Dan. 9:4–19), we will discover that it would take us perhaps five minutes to say this prayer. Or we might think of the longest of the psalms, Psalm 119, which might take twenty or thirty minutes to say aloud.

We can acknowledge that sometimes our prayers might be longer than the Lord's Prayer; we will address the issue of length, of extended prayer times and periods of fasting, at a later place in our study. But the point we need to grasp now is this: brief prayers are pleasing to the Lord; brief prayers are heard and answered by him readily and gladly. Length is not what makes a prayer acceptable to God.

A SIMPLE PRAYER

Second, we observe that the prayer Jesus teaches is very simple. It does not have long, impressive sentences, nor does it have deep theological complexity as its character. It is a brief series of straightforward statements and requests. This surprises some of us, who might honestly believe that we must make more complex what Jesus declares to be so simple! "Surely it cannot be that easy!" we say to ourselves. "Prayer must be more profound, more eloquent, more taxing than this little model that Jesus gives us!"

Again, we need to ask ourselves why we might make such a statement. If the answer centers on our feeling better about ourselves when we pray prayers that we assess as theologically deep and verbally impressive, then we are again profoundly wrong. Prayer is not a performance in which we are trying to prove something to God about our depth of theological understanding or our skills of eloquence. Nor is prayer a performance in which we seek to impress our fellow believers about these things. And prayer is certainly not a performance in which we are to appraise and applaud ourselves for theological acumen or verbal gymnastics. Prayer is talking to God; prayer is not about trying to feel better about ourselves. Most of the time, of course, we are not quite so foolish as to judge our prayers in such ways.

Yet a problem remains: many of us struggle with thinking that others may view us as unspiritual if we pray in public, or if we admit to praying in private, prayers that are brief and simple. Indeed, many Christians are deeply reluctant to ever pray in front of others for fear of what others may think. But it is very sad that many believers feel this way, and some of us have been very sinful in making other Christians feel ashamed of their own prayers. Jesus encourages us all to know that prayer is communicating to God in the way that he teaches us. Prayer is not about demonstrating to others our spirituality, our theological understanding, or our verbal ability. Our prayers can be brief and they can be simple.

A PLAIN PRAYER

Third, prayer can be plain, as is the Lord's Prayer. This prayer that Jesus teaches us is so ordinary! I do not mean this as a criticism, nor to deny the beauty of the Lord's Prayer. I want to try to communicate that this is another major area in which we become confused about prayer. We think that our prayers must be more involved, and somehow more intense, than these plain phrases of praise and request that Jesus teaches us. "It surely can't be quite that ordinary!" we think to ourselves. "It must be necessary for our prayers to have an extraordinary character! Doesn't there have to be more fervency, passion, and emotional intensity than is present in Jesus' plain petitions?"

How are these questions to be answered? Sometimes there will be fervency, passion, and emotional intensity in our prayers. It is fine to express this emotion in our prayers if it truly reflects the way we feel.

Think of the prayer of the tax collector. He beat his breast and would not lift up his eyes to heaven when he prayed: "God, be merciful to me, a sinner!" (Luke 18:13). Or think about Jesus' brief prayers from the cross; they are certainly full of passion! Many psalms and other prayers (for example, some of the prayers of Jeremiah, both in the book of Jeremiah and in Lamentations, or the prayer of Hannah in 1 Samuel 2) are fervent and passionate, but they arise from situations in which the one praying is indeed in distress. In some of his prayers, Jeremiah is deeply troubled about the destruction of Jerusalem by the Babylonians. In others, he is distressed because the Lord does not seem to be listening to him. Hannah is barren, longs to have a child, and must deal with the ridicule of her rival, Peninnah. In such cases, emotional intensity is a natural response to the pressure of the circumstances facing these believers.

It is the same for us: when someone we love—a spouse, child, or dear friend—is desperately ill, we cry out to the Lord in anguish. When my wife, Vicki, was diagnosed with colon cancer a decade ago and the chemotherapy was ravaging her body, I prayed many intense, passionate prayers—mostly very short! "Lord, do something!" "Lord, listen!" God, of course, encourages us to bring our intense pain or pleasure to him, and he assures us that he will hear with compassion or gladness, as the case may be. Yet there are several significant issues to notice.

First, it is not the emotional intensity of our prayers that makes God attentive to them. He listens intently and attentively because he loves us, not because of the passion with which we pray to him. We need to be reminded of this, for we very readily judge ourselves, and others, about the quality or value of our prayer life, and the criterion we use for this judgment is often the emotional fervor or the experiential strength of our feelings when we pray.

I do not wish to deny that sometimes Christians have wonderful moments of feeling the Lord's presence when we are praying. In addition, on rare occasions we may have extended periods of acutely sensing his love for us, or his grief over our sins, or his comfort in our sorrows, or his power at work when we teach his Word or otherwise serve him.

The important point, however, is that we do not begin to measure the validity of our prayers, or the maturity of our spirituality, by the depth, height, or power of our experience. If we do such measuring, all sorts of dangers can arise. For example, we might start feeling proud of our experience, as if we had a closer relationship with the Lord than that enjoyed by our fellow believers. Jesus warned his disciples against such pride when he reminded them to rejoice that their names were written in heaven, rather than in the excitement of having experienced the Father powerfully at work in answer to their prayers (Luke 10:20).

An additional problem is that if we are not careful when we openly share such "experiences" we have had with the Lord, we can make other believers who have not had them start doubting the reality of their own relationship with God. Paul addresses this problem in Colossians chapter 2 when he encourages the believers not to be robbed of their confidence in Christ by fellow Christians who stand on visions and other spiritual experiences they have had (Col. 2:18–19).

What tends to happen very easily is that when the Lord grants us some special experience, we start boasting about it, as if this were a mark of our own spiritual maturity rather than a particular gift of God. Because we are all such sinners who are so easily seduced by pride, we also struggle with wanting to feel superior to other Christians. In addition, we may want to keep having the same experience ourselves so that we can walk by sight rather than by faith. So we try to manufacture the experience to make it keep happening, or we tell stories about it to prove to others how close to the Lord we are and what prayer warriors we have become.

I recall a pastor's sharing, during a sermon, about a one-day prayer retreat he had taken the previous week. He told us all what a day of sweet fellowship he had enjoyed with the Lord, how rapidly the day had gone by, how easily he had spent hours in prayer. The effect of this story, I am afraid, was one of two things: some present were amazed by the pastor's spirituality, and put him on a pedestal as a spiritual giant whose experience was utterly unlike their own; others simply thought he was telling a complete fabrication and stopped believing anything he said about personal spirituality.

The heart of the problem, I believe, was that the pastor was claiming to have spent a day walking by sight—experiencing the Lord so personally and directly that it was as if he and the Lord were walking arm in arm together through the woods all day without any interruption. The truth is that the New Testament teaches us that we are called to walk by faith now rather than by sight, and so we must be content with not always, or with only rarely, or maybe even not at all, having intense experiences of the Lord's presence.

The day will come, thank God, when faith will be turned to sight. Then we will see Christ face to face, and we as his redeemed people will indeed walk through the woods and gardens with him—as did Adam and Eve before the fall. In the meantime, however, we do not walk by sight, and the passion of our hearts is no trustworthy measure of the reality of our prayers, nor is our passion a measure of the willingness of our Father to hear us.

This brings up a second and related point. Less emotionally intense prayers are heard just as readily by God as the most passionate prayers we pray. We are encouraged to pray about many things that are not, or are not immediately, matters of life and death: our daily food, our need to grow in love and in virtue, our desire for our children's well-being and for their future, and many other regular needs. It is not only the urgent, desperate problems that God is willing to hear and to answer. We can bring anything to our heavenly Father! And we can come to him just as we are, whether we are in a time of great sorrow or joy, or whether it is just an ordinary, uneventful day.

A third issue is that we can begin to think that the intensity and fervor of our prayers, or our perseverance in prayer, are placing the Lord God under obligation to answer our prayers. It is as if we were saying to him: "Lord, I have prayed about this issue with such passion. I have prayed about it every day for seventy days. Now you must answer me, because I deserve it."

You may wish to deny that you are ever so crass and manipulative in your approach to the Lord, but it is my experience that I often behave this way—and so, I suspect, do all other believers. We all too easily begin to think that the Lord is in our debt. We start believing that our faithfulness, our intensity, or our persistence in prayer requires the Lord to answer in the way we desire.

But this notion of the Lord's indebtedness to us is not what he teaches us about prayer. Prayer is our response to God, the God who graciously invites us to come to him with our thanksgiving and requests. He is never indebted to us; we are always indebted to him. We cannot manipulate him into a position where we can make him answer us—no matter how much time, how much emotional energy, how much spiritual fervor, or how much frequency of prayer we offer to him. We are always beggars who are completely dependent on his generous kindness to us. We are not those who can bargain with him on the basis of our perceived spiritual power or faithfulness.

A CONFIDENT PRAYER

This brings us to a fourth central matter that Jesus teaches us when he gives us the Lord's Prayer. Little children who know they are loved by their parents or grandparents and who are fully secure in their love do not have to try to impress their fathers, their mothers, or their grandparents. So it is with God. He is "Our Father." We are indeed loved by him. We can be secure in the knowledge of his love. We do not have to try to impress him with our prayers. So Jesus teaches us to pray with confidence, to approach God directly with a sense of security and call him "Father!" or "Our Father!" God is always "open" for such prayers. He never rests, but rather is always at work, listening to our prayers and eager to meet our needs.

Our confidence and directness pleases God, for it shows that we are coming to him as little children to a father, a mother, or a grandparent. We are coming to the Lord knowing that we are loved and that he will gladly hear us. To put this point another way, we are coming to the Father as those who believe the gospel of Christ. For the gospel teaches us that the God who made the heavens and the earth has made himself our Father through his Son, Jesus, by taking away all our failure, idolatry, unbelief, and shame through his death for us on the cross.

In order to make very clear this matter of the confidence we can have in prayer, I will tell a brief story about one of my grandsons. One of my daughters-in-law is French, and her children call me "Papy"—the French term for "Grandfather." I remember that when one of them was three, I would sometimes answer the phone to this beloved little voice: "Papy, I love you! I want you to come and have dinner with us." I would say, "Yes! Thank you! Mamy and I will come. I love you, too." (Of course, I would then telephone our son or daughter-in-law to double-check, because sometimes they did not know that he was inviting us—this was his idea completely.)

My grandson would say these few words and then put the phone down. I was delighted, of course! He did not need to say anything else. His brief words, his simple and straightforward expression of love, his request—these were enough for me. If that is how I, a sinner, respond, then how much more does our perfect God delight in his children's simple, brief, plain expressions of love and our requests for his presence and help in our lives! We can tell him happily, and we can tell him often, how much we love him, need him, and long to be with him. Our model, the Lord's Prayer, teaches us that we can say these things briefly, simply, plainly, and confidently.

Questions for Reflection and Discussion

1. Do you think of yourself as someone who has a great prayer life, as being poor at prayer, or as falling somewhere in between?

2. Were you troubled, encouraged, or a bit of both by my confession of my own spiritual poverty at the beginning of this first chapter?

3. Do you find it encouraging that the disciples came to Jesus to ask him to teach them to pray?

4. Have you ever asked either the Lord or a fellow believer, "Can you teach me how to pray?"

5. Do you sometimes struggle with feeling that short, simple, plain prayers are not very spiritual? What might you say to yourself when you feel like this?

6. For you, what are the barriers in coming to God in prayer? Why do you find prayer difficult?

7. Have you felt the need to get yourself straightened out spiritually or into the right frame of mind before you could pray "real" prayers?

8. Do you sometimes want to judge the value of your prayers? If you do, what criteria have you used for judging their value? What do you say to yourself to refrain from doing this?

2

THE CONTENT OF
THE LORD'S PRAYER

Luke 11:2b–4

Father, hallowed be your name.
   Your kingdom come.
   Give us each day our daily bread,
   and forgive us our sins,
      for we ourselves forgive everyone who is
      indebted to us.
   And lead us not into temptation.

What does Jesus teach us to pray? He begins with "Father, hallowed be your name."

PRAISE

Jesus encourages us always to include praise in our prayers. He wants us to reflect on the reasons why we should "hallow" God's name. Each time I pray, I need to ask myself: "What do I know about God that gives me reasons to honor him? What aspects of his character do I particularly delight in? What is there about his work in this world that makes me glad to know that he is its Author, Maker, and Provider?" Again, I will give a very personal example. When my father came to faith in Christ at the age of seventy-five, just six weeks before his death, I was thankful: "Praise you, Lord, for saving my dad!" But because I have a doubting heart, I also had to add: "May his conversion be genuine! Forgive my unbelief!" Today as I write this, I am contemplating an e-mail I just received from a young couple whose wedding I performed a couple of years ago, with a picture of their firstborn who came into this world yesterday. "Thank you, Lord, for this little baby."

When we take time to pray, we are to ask ourselves where we have seen the Lord at work in our lives, to think about what aspects of his love and power displayed in creation and redemption fill us with joy. Jesus is teaching us to stop and to consider why we worship God when we come to him to pray. What is it about this day, about this marriage, this family, this friendship, this situation, this meal, these moments of worship, this workplace, this particular time and situation for which I should remember to be thankful? In this and in many other things, little children can lead us with their directness and lack of pretension. My little granddaughter, who likes to pray at mealtimes, will add whatever is special to her at the moment. So at one meal after her mother's prayer, she added: "And thank you, Lord, for raspberries!"

In human relationships, saying "thank you" or expressing appreciation for the loving-kindness or faithful work of one's wife or husband, parents, children, friends, or workmates is an integral part of living together, and of building warmth and depth of love into a relationship. People need to know that they are loved and that we do not take them for granted. We need to tell them that we appreciate what they do for us, and above all, we need to tell them how much we appreciate them for themselves. Just so with the Lord: part of our growing in love for him, part of our developing a deeper and warmer fellowship with him, is saying "thank you" and honoring him for all the good things he does for us—and above all, for who he is.

OUR NEED FOR THE COMING OF THE KINGDOM

After a word of praise, Jesus comes to our requests: "Your kingdom come." (In Matthew he adds: "Your will be done, on earth as it is in heaven" [Matt. 6:10].) Jesus comes quickly to the matter of our needs. We usually start with them! He urges us to pray for the coming of the kingdom—for God's will to be done on earth as it is in heaven.

Jesus is reminding us that our first longing should be for God's just and merciful rule to be realized here on earth. Do you long for the kingdom to come? Do you long for everything to be set right, for evil to be banished from the earth, for sickness, sorrow, and death to be destroyed? First, we can think about the coming of the kingdom among those we love.

I remember returning a year or so ago with my wife, Vicki, after spending three weeks with her parents. At that time, her dad was struggling with some form of senile dementia. Dementia is a sad business. I prayed often: "Lord, please take Dad into your kingdom, peacefully, soon!" Dad is fully in the kingdom now; we miss him, and we know that Mom misses him even more. We pray: "Grant Mom the comfort of your kingdom." We all have family needs like this—areas of need for the reality of the coming of the kingdom.

Then we can think about the need for the coming of the kingdom in those areas of trouble in the world around us. We all hear the daily news from Iraq. Soldiers and civilians keep dying there. We all long for this war to be over; we hope and pray for peace. We pray for the defeat of terrorism and the end of suicide bombing.

In addition, we can pray for the coming of the kingdom in those areas of our lives where we are experiencing particular struggles. Jesus wants us to look at our lives and then ask: "Where do I see things not as they should be? Where do I long to see change? Where do I long to see sin overthrown? Where do I wish to see life as it will be when Jesus returns?" Jesus encourages us: "Pray about those things. Pray about the coming of the kingdom in your own life day by day."

Each day I need to ask myself: "Where does the kingdom need to come in my life today?" Try to imagine that you are already in the presence of Christ and that his kingdom is fully established, both across this world and in your own life. You are made perfect! Now think about what this would mean for you, and ask yourself the question: "What would it mean for my life today for me to live with the firstfruits of what I will be one day?" Then pray that the kingdom would begin to come in your life now. That is what Jesus desires for us to pray.

DAILY BREAD

The next petition is about our personal everyday needs: "Give us each day our daily bread." We should not be ashamed or reluctant to ask God for the ordinary needs and wants of our daily lives. To survive, we need food and drink. We need clothing and housing. We need work and income. We need rest and leisure. God is a generous God. He has created a bountiful world. He loves to "richly provide[] us with everything to enjoy" (1 Tim. 6:17). Jesus is not an ascetic; that is, Jesus does not think that it is virtuous to deny ourselves food, or drink, or marriage, or children, or beauty, or sleep, or health, or anything else in creation—as if the rejection of the good things made by God had some value in and of itself.

That last passage may trouble some. If you find those words problematic, then hear these much stronger words from the apostle Paul:

> Now the Spirit expressly says that in later times some will depart from the faith by devoting themselves to deceitful spirits and teachings of demons, through the insincerity of liars whose consciences are seared, who forbid marriage and require abstinence from foods that God created to be received with thanksgiving by those who believe and know the truth. For everything created by God is good, and nothing is to be rejected if it is received with thanksgiving, for it is made holy by the word of God and prayer. (1 Tim. 4:1–5)

Paul tells us very plainly that the denial of the gift of marriage and food is a doctrine of demons taught by liars. The same is true of any suggestion that it is more spiritual to go without beauty, or music, or laughter, or happiness, or food, or work, or play, or exercise, or any other ordinary part of created human life. God created this world, and he designed our human life to be lived in this world. He simply wants us to be thankful. He declared it good at creation—he said so, over and over again. (See the repeated refrain "it was good" in Genesis 1.) Just think, for an example, about the profligacy of spring!

The Lord truly does not think it is virtuous, or more spiritual, for us to go without or to have only the bare necessities of life. The Lord is no ascetic who wants us to demonstrate our spirituality by denying ourselves good things—as if there were some spiritual virtue in such denial for its own sake. The virtue and the spirituality of such self-denial is what almost all human religion has taught—that we become more spiritual, and draw closer to God, by cultivating a lack of interest in the ordinary blessings and joys of life. That may be the teaching of much humanly devised religious practice, and of many programs for spiritual discipline and growth, but it is not the teaching of God's Word. It is not the gospel of Christ!

Jesus does not consider people more godly if they don't have enough to eat, fresh water to drink, clean water to bathe in, or a place to sleep—for example, the people enduring the aftermath of a disaster such as Hurricane Katrina. The Lord sees such deprivation as a consequence of the fall, and part of the curse on our world. He does not see such troubles as a mark of spirituality, though of course he is filled with sorrow and compassion for those who are deprived and suffering in such ways. His sorrow and compassion is a response to their lack of the good things that he delights to give to all the people of this world.

The Lord desires that we reflect on the richness of our life, on the beauty of the countryside in which we may be privileged to live, on the majesty of the stars in the night sky, on the good food we have to eat, on the joys of daily life and of human relationships, and on every other good thing there is in this world. God cheerfully gives these to us for our enjoyment. He happily encourages us to come to him with our most mundane needs. It is not "unspiritual" to ask for such things.

Of course, we must remember that this prayer is inclusive of others—it is not "all about me." We pray: "Give *us* each day *our* daily bread." Am I praying for the needs of others as well as for my own needs and those of my immediate family? In this "me"-centered culture, we very easily start praying only for our own needs and desires. Praying for our needs, however, should immediately bring to mind the Lord's generosity—and so we should be praying for his gracious kindness to others as well as ourselves. We should be asking God to meet the urgent daily needs of the victims of the latest disaster, and of those racked by war, and of others in great need—as well as for him to provide the daily necessities that are a part of all our lives.

FORGIVENESS FOR OUR SINS

Jesus then asks us to pray: "Forgive us our sins." Just as we pray for each day's food, so each one of us must daily come to God and confess our failures. Whenever we come to him, it is appropriate to have a sense of our unworthiness, just like the tax collector who prayed: "God, be merciful to me, a sinner!" (Luke 18:13). This does not mean that we are to lose the sense of assurance and ease in coming to God that is at the heart of what Jesus is teaching in the Lord's Prayer. It is precisely because we know that he is eager to receive us that we can come to him just as we are, with all our shortcomings.

This is true in human relationships as well. The better the marriage, the happier the home, the closer the friendship, the easier it is to be honest and open with each other because we know that we are loved, forgiven, and accepted. My wife knows me better than anyone else apart from the Lord, but I am comfortable and at home with her, even with all my weaknesses, because she knows them, she forgives them, and she loves me anyway! Just so with the Lord: he knows us fully and accepts us wholeheartedly in his beloved Son.

But because we can come to the Lord without fear, we should also come to him honestly, acknowledging the particular areas of sin, of coldness of heart, and of lack of faithfulness that make up our lives. Where am I failing to love God with my whole being and failing to love my neighbor today? Just considering our shortcomings with regard to those two great commandments would make for a long list! We should remember that the Lord wants us to be specific, for it is only as we face up to the practical reality of our failing to love God and to love our neighbor that we begin to see the seriousness of our sins. Sin is a nasty and ugly business—the truth is that every day we grieve the Lord and we hurt the people around us. Only reflection and confession will help us to take our sins seriously.

Jesus teaches us to pray: "Forgive *us our* sins." When I acknowledge my failures and my disobedience, I know that I am one with every other member of the human race. Everyone else is a sinner like me—and so there are "group sins." All of us need to pray for the forgiveness of sins committed as individuals, but we also need to pray about the sins committed along with our fellows. What sins am I involved with that I am committing with others—sins of gossip, of greed, of group pride, of arrogance, of racial prejudice, of idolatry, and of unbelief?

All of us belong to families, work or study settings, and churches that have their particular "institutional sins," which we become engaged in without being much aware of them, for they are simply part of the scenery in which we live. We must cultivate sensitivity about these sins, too. In America we are all bound up in a culture that idolizes "me" and personal fulfillment and happiness. How has this powerful god caught me in its spell, so that I am unfaithful, along with all other Americans, to God on high?

In addition, I need to ask whether I should pray for the repentance of particular people around me. I am not encouraging us to focus on the sins of others rather than our own sins, but exhorting us to pray for those who sin against us—just as Jesus commands us: "Bless those who curse you, pray for those who abuse you" (Luke 6:28; see also Matt. 5:44).

This is a challenging issue, for often we would far rather nurse our animosity and resentment against others for their sins toward us. But the Lord's plan is different. He tells us that as soon as we think of those who sin against us, then we are to have a sense of urgency about praying for their forgiveness and for their repentance. Think of Jesus praying from the cross: "Father, forgive them!" Can we pray like that? If we do pray like Jesus, it will stop us from harboring anger and bitterness toward those who treat us poorly. When we start praying for people, we must begin to stop hating them! Many believers have very difficult people in their extended families. Sometimes these people can behave very selfishly, meanly, and even cruelly. They can cause great pain to us or to someone we love. It is easy in such a situation to develop a settled anger and dislike for the person—and feel quite justified in hating him or her, maybe even praying that God will judge the person with death, soon! But the Lord does not want us to dislike people—even those who hate us, who curse us, who treat us poorly. He does not desire that we pray that he would judge them. Rather, he rebukes us when we have such ugly passions, by reminding us of his patient and forgiving love for us. He asks us to begin to pray for those who are unkind, ungrateful, and even wicked. He also asks us to pray for him to help us to begin to love our enemies, and for him to enable us to be a blessing to them. The Lord delights to answer such prayers, for this is how he himself loved us when we were still his enemies.

FORGIVING OTHERS

As we pray for forgiveness for ourselves, Jesus reminds us that we are to remember to be forgiving to others: "Forgive us our sins, for we ourselves forgive everyone who is indebted to us." Jesus is challenging us to reflect on this question: "How can I truly ask for, and receive, the mercy of God for my own failures if I am not prepared to extend that mercy to others?" The hardness of heart that refuses to forgive others indicates that I really have no true sense of the seriousness of my own sin. If I reply to this question, "But forgiveness is difficult and costly" (which it most certainly is), then I demonstrate that I have not comprehended the difficulty and cost to God of forgiving my sins. For God to forgive us was enormously costly. He gave his Son up to death for my constant sinning, for my abuse of his patience and kindness, for my cold heart and my selfish will, for my worship of many idols, for my constant lack of true faith, and for the poverty of my love for him, or for anyone else.

Each one reading this can readily imagine a difficult personal example; all of us are familiar with people who take advantage of any sign of kindness and generosity. But as you think about even the most unpleasant person you know, remember that his or her abuse of and taking advantage of you is no worse than your constant abuse of the Lord and your taking advantage of his daily and constant kindness and generosity to you.

The reality, of course, is that all of us find it easier to ask forgiveness for ourselves than to extend forgiveness to others. Jesus is reminding us of the imperative of understanding our own need and the cost to God of forgiving us, so that we may remember to ask him to help us to forgive. As we cry out for his help to forgive, so we will begin to be merciful to others, for our hearts will be more and more touched and changed by the knowledge of his mercy to us.

If I have a hard and unforgiving heart toward anyone today, then I am to take it to the Lord in prayer; I am to meditate on the forgiveness he has shown me; I am to think about the cost of his mercy to me; and I am to be prepared to count the cost of forgiving that troublesome person!

As Christian believers, we regularly take the Lord's Supper together. Jesus tells us: "And whenever you stand praying, forgive, if you have anything against anyone, so that your Father also who is in heaven may forgive you your trespasses" (Mark 11:25). I need to come to his Table remembering that the Lord gladly forgives me everything! The Lord tells me that if someone has something against me, I should go to that person and make peace, rather than thinking that I can come to the Lord's Table and carry on my relationship with him without concerning myself with difficult human problems between myself and others (Matt. 5:23–24). God is at peace with me, through Jesus, and he calls me to give others his kiss of peace.

TEMPTATION

In Luke's version of the prayer, Jesus' final petition is this: "And lead us not into temptation." We need to be strengthened for the battle against sin. God knows our weaknesses; he knows the areas in which we struggle; he knows where we are likely to fall—so we should bring to him those very things. Jesus wants us each day to be aware of the particular battle lines in our lives. What are the areas in which I need to fight against sin and put it to death? Is my problem today gossip, an unforgiving heart, discouragement, pride, bitterness, self-pity, sexual temptation, a lazy streak, anger, or coldness toward others? Each one of us can answer with several of these sins and more! Jesus encourages us to bring these particular temptations to our Father in heaven for his help. He is eager to help us in our fight against sin. Are we concerned enough about the seriousness of this conflict with sin that we will come to him with our specific needs, asking for his strength and help in resisting these temptations?

This brief and simple prayer is Jesus' answer to his disciples' request for help. If we want to learn to pray, here is our model:

> Father, hallowed be your name.
> > Your kingdom come.
> > Give us each day our daily bread,
> > and forgive us our sins,
> > > for we ourselves forgive everyone who is indebted to us.
> > And lead us not into temptation.

Prayer truly is this simple! We don't have to attend seminary to learn to pray. We don't need to take a Ph.D., an M.A., or a B.A. in prayer, or even "Prayer 101" or a high school diploma in prayer. Jesus' lesson on prayer is more at the kindergarten, or even preschool, level. It is not necessary for us to spend hours on our knees in order to be heard by God. We don't have to work ourselves up into some special spiritual frame of mind. We don't have to get our lives sorted out before we pray. We simply have to come. God promises to hear us when we come in all our need—just as Jesus instructs us.

Questions for Reflection and Discussion

1. Do you sometimes use the Lord's Prayer as a model for your own prayers? How does this work on a practical level? Do you find a particular pattern helpful?

2. Do you sometimes pray the Lord's Prayer just as it is? Do you find problems with doing this?

3. What praise will you include in your prayers as you follow Jesus' pattern of beginning a prayer by hallowing the Father's name?

4. At this time in your life, where do you need to pray for the kingdom to come?

5. What daily needs do you have in your life right now?

6. What do you see to be the areas of greatest need for forgiveness in your life?

7. Do you find certain people difficult to forgive? How will you deal with this problem?

8. What are the areas of your greatest struggles with temptation at this stage of your life?

9. As you look at the simple statements in the Lord's Prayer as it is found in Luke 11, which part or parts of it do you tend to leave out of your own prayers? Why do you think you omit these parts?

3

TWO STORIES ABOUT PRAYER

Luke 11:5–13

Our discussion of the Lord's Prayer brings us to Jesus' additional teaching about prayer in Luke chapter 11. It is evident from the context that Jesus is trying to help his disciples understand more about the prayer he has just taught to them. He gives us some stories or illustrations about prayer and some words of invitation to prayer. Both the stories he tells and his invitations to prayer are intended as an encouragement to us.

A FRIEND AT MIDNIGHT

Which of you who has a friend will go to him at midnight and say to him, "Friend, lend me three loaves, for a friend of mine has arrived on a journey, and I have nothing to set before him"; and he will answer from within, "Do not bother me; the door is now shut, and my children are with me in bed. I cannot get up and give you anything"? I tell you,

though he will not get up and give him anything
because he is his friend, yet because of his impudence he will rise and give him whatever he needs.
(Luke 11:5–8)

This first story is delightful. We read it and immediately picture the scene in our minds: the man coming at
midnight to try to arouse his friend, and the half-awake
grumbling from within. Whenever I read it I think of visiting a friend in Heidelberg, Germany, almost forty years
ago. Three of us—my wife and I and a friend—were driving from L'Abri in Switzerland, and we had been invited
to stay the night with a beloved friend in Heidelberg. For
various reasons we were delayed on the road; we finally
arrived at the apartment building in which our friend
lived just before midnight. When we figured out which
apartment was his (all the lights were out), we had to
throw pebbles up to the third-floor window to wake him.
By then it was midnight exactly—the city clocks were
chiming twelve!

Thankfully, we chose the right apartment window to
"stone"—and thankfully, we did not break the window! Our
friend had to get up, come down, unlock the front door, and
lead us in. Then he had to find some food at that late hour
and sort out sleeping arrangements, towels, and everything
else to get us settled. This was long before the days of cell
phones, so we had been unable to alert him of our many
hours of delay. He had given up on our coming long before,
assuming that we had decided against the visit.

The most amusing part of the story was the next morning at breakfast. As was his custom, after we had eaten,
our friend read from a collection of Scripture readings for
each morning and evening of the year. The reading for that

particular day was this passage from Luke 11! (See *Daily Light on the Daily Path* for the morning of June 7.)

We felt we were being "impudent" to wake our friend up at that time of night, in a strange town, not being quite sure of the window, not wanting to wake up others, and not wanting to break his window! Would he welcome us? We were very embarrassed when he appeared. Relieved as well, but mostly embarrassed. Jesus, of course, draws our attention to this aspect of the friend's behavior: "Because of [the man's] impudence [NIV: "boldness"] he will rise and give him whatever he needs."

Why does Jesus tell this story, and why does he stress the "impudence" or "boldness"? Jesus is teaching all of us, all his disciples, that we can be bold, even impudent, in our praying. We don't need to be afraid to come to God, as if he were a person we must be careful not to disturb, or around whom we must tread on tiptoes and speak with care.

In addition, we can come to the Lord at any time—we don't have to wait for a propitious moment, or be worried that he might be out of temper, or asleep, or too busy. Even if the time seems embarrassing to us, we may be sure that God will listen. He does not get tired. He never sleeps. He is not too busy.

We are to feel free to come to him with any request, no matter how little it may seem (three small loaves of bread is not a major favor for which to ask). The Lord is not weighing the great need of our prayers in a balance. He is not thinking: "All my time and attention is filled by matters far more significant than the petty affairs of Jerram Barrs." He is not preoccupied with the prayers of people who are more important than we are, as if he were unable to put aside time to hear us patiently. We can be bold at any moment of the day or night, at any time in our lives, about any little need that we may have. That is the point of this story.

INVITATION TO PRAY

> And I tell you, ask, and it will be given to you; seek, and you will find; knock, and it will be opened to you. For everyone who asks receives, and the one who seeks finds, and to the one who knocks it will be opened. (Luke 11:9–10)

Jesus follows his first story with these three encouraging words: "Ask, seek, knock." Each encouraging word is accompanied by a promise. And then the promise is repeated. It is as if we were too slow to take in Jesus' assuring words the first time. And of course we are too slow! We all need to hear this encouragement, and these promises, repeated over and over again.

Why are we so slow to learn that we can indeed take Jesus' words to heart, that we can trust his words completely, and that we can act on them? I think the answer is related to the confusions about prayer that I was addressing in the first chapter. We are slow to believe that prayer can be this simple and this straightforward. It is almost as if we wanted prayer to be more difficult. It is as if we wanted prayer to have more to do with the supposed state of our spiritual maturity than with the ease of coming to God with anything at any time. It is as if we wanted prayer to depend more fully on us: on our long prayers, on our faith, on our strength of devotion, on our passion, on our well-expressed thoughts, on our theological wisdom.

Jesus assures us, however, that prayer is indeed this simple: "Ask, and it will be given to you; seek, and you will find; knock, and it will be opened to you." Later in this book we will address this question more fully—that is, why might we want prayer to be more difficult than it really is?

GOOD FATHERS

> What father among you, if his son asks for a fish, will instead of a fish give him a serpent; or if he asks for an egg, will give him a scorpion? If you then, who are evil, know how to give good gifts to your children, how much more will the heavenly Father give the Holy Spirit to those who ask him! (Luke 11:11–13)

On this occasion of teaching the Lord's Prayer, Jesus gives a final illustration of a child's asking a father for some food. Again, it is a simple picture, one repeated every day in millions of homes around the world: children asking their parents for food. What could be more mundane than this, more ordinary and more unexceptional?

That is exactly Jesus' point! Every day our children ask us for food. How do we respond? Always positively, every day, day after day, week after week, month after month, year after year. We never give them a snake instead of a fish, or a scorpion for breakfast instead of an egg! Care and provision for our children come naturally to us. Anything else is unthinkable. We generally do this gladly.

Even when we are tired, sick, distressed, anxious, grieving, or bad-tempered, we still feed our children every day. Suppose we are in a foul mood because of a hard day at work, or in response to a difficult drive home because of someone else's road rage. We still answer our children's demand for food. Perhaps we are angry with them because they have behaved badly. Still, we do not give them meals that will harm or poison them; rather, we feed them well.

Yet as Jesus points out, we who give these good gifts to our children are evil. Think of the awful thoughts that every one of us sometimes has toward our children, even if we might never express them openly and even if we are deeply ashamed of these thoughts as soon as we have them. We have all heard mothers and fathers yelling unkind, mean, and hurtful words at their children in public. We have even heard men and women curse their kids and treat them in ways that make us want to stop our ears and weep for the child who is treated so abominably.

But if we are honest with ourselves, we have all sometimes felt such anger in our hearts toward our own children—even though these thoughts rarely, or never, escape our internal conversations. We are indeed evil, though such a description of us as parents may offend us. Yet we, who are evil, do provide for our children. When a parent does not provide good food, or when a parent poisons or mistreats a child, we are appalled because we know that such behavior is unnatural, abominable, and thoroughly wicked.

We occasionally hear or read of such awful examples. I know a couple who graduated from Covenant Theological Seminary and who now serve in pastoral ministry. I met the little girl they have adopted. She had been left in a crib for three years—with no washing, no words of love, no attention, just scraps of food thrown in from time to time. I read another shocking example in the book *Nature Noir*.[1] The author, a park ranger, describes seeing a man who threw his baby, as if the child were a baseball, through the window of a rapidly moving car driven by the child's mother. She was leaving the child with the father because she was angry with him, and wanted him to care for the child. But the father was so self-centered and so angry with the mother, and had so little interest in caring for his child, that with no regard at all for the child's safety or even the child's life, he simply threw the child like a ball.

When we hear stories like these, our reaction is to boil with rage, and to long for some appropriate punishment for those who practice such abuse toward their own children. Almost all human beings see such behavior as deeply wicked and abhorrently unnatural—so much so that we think that a person who behaves like this does not deserve the label "human."

But this is precisely Jesus' point. If it is so natural and obvious and right for us, even though we ourselves are evil, to care for our children in good and appropriate ways, how much more will our holy heavenly Father care for us! Jesus is laboring hard to get his teaching about prayer into our heads and hearts. God is good. He is a Father to us. He does care about us. We can come to him every day with any need we have—just like a child needing food several times a day. He will gladly listen and answer us. He will meet our needs and come to our aid.

THE HOLY SPIRIT

> How much more will the heavenly Father give the
> Holy Spirit to those who ask him! (Luke 11:13)

Why does Jesus choose to mention the Holy Spirit at this point in his teaching? The appearance of Jesus' words about the Holy Spirit does seem like a sudden shift in the focus of his words about prayer. The answer to this question will take us back to the beginning of Jesus' teaching on the subject. If we think back to the Lord's Prayer, the majority of the petitions have to do with our need for our lives to be put right. One petition is about our daily food, but the others are about our spiritual hunger: our obligation to honor God, the requirement to have his kingdom realized in our lives, our need for forgiveness, our calling to forgive others, and the pressures of temptation that we constantly face.

In all these petitions, we need to ask for the help of God's Holy Spirit. We will not hallow God's name without the Spirit's softening our hard hearts and reminding us of the good gifts that we daily enjoy from our heavenly Father. We will not experience the righteousness of God's rule in our lives without the Spirit's transforming help. We will not seek God's mercy for our failures each day without the Spirit's conviction. We will not realize how unforgiving we are without the Spirit's recalling to us the forbearance and patience of the Father. We will not turn away from temptation unless the Spirit makes our consciences sensitive.

More than any physical necessity for which we come to God in prayer, we should be asking for the Spirit to help us. Jesus reminds us of this, and assures us that just as we meet our children's needs, so God will meet his children's needs. In fact, he will help us much more than we help our children, for he is completely good, whereas we are evil.

Where is the focus of our prayers? Is it our material needs? God knows about these material needs, and he certainly encourages us to bring them to him—I do not wish to deemphasize that fact in any way. But we all have so many other needs about which we are often unaware. Jesus desires that we become sensitive to these other needs (the need to hunger and thirst for righteousness, for example), and he urges us to pray about these needs, too. He promises help, without any qualification, without any ifs, ands, or buts.

Jesus teaches us that the Father is always ready to hear his children's prayers. He is never tired or distracted, nor is he too busy when we come to him. This is true even when we bring to him our ordinary daily needs for food, health, and rest. Jesus emphasizes this readiness of the Father to listen to our needs; he underlines it with stories and with direct promises. He finishes his teaching on prayer, on the occasion recorded for us in Luke chapter 11, with a story about a father's feeding his child rather than giving him a poisonous snake or deadly scorpion. Jesus purposely gives an unthinkable and shocking example to drive his point home. If we who are evil would not think of harming our children when they are hungry, how much more can we be certain that God, who is always and only good, will come to our aid when we are in need of the Holy Spirit? The Lord's Prayer is primarily about our spiritual needs, and Jesus is teaching us that when we come to God, aware of our need for the Holy Spirit, we may be sure that he will always answer, "Yes!"

Questions for Reflection and Discussion

1. Do you have a favorite story that you like to tell about some "happy coincidence" in your life that gives you good memories of God's care for you?

2. Are there stories from your life that you might share of a friend's opening his or her home and being hospitable to you even though it was inconvenient to your friend—or of your opening your home to someone else when it was inconvenient for you?

3. As you reflect on these stories that Jesus tells, what is most precious to you about the ways in which you have experienced God's fatherly care?

4. Thinking about your life now, in what areas do you want to ask, seek, and knock? What do you especially desire God to do for you?

5. When you hear this text, do you find Jesus' words about our being evil jarring or uncomfortable in any way? Can you acknowledge in your heart to the Lord that even your most precious relationships, like that of parent and child, reveal ample evidence of the evil within you, though you might never act it out in some appalling manner?

6. Each one of us has seen examples of parents' not caring for their children. Have you found any particular examples especially shocking? Did seeing or hearing these examples affect you in your own behavior—challenging you never to behave in such a way yourself?

7. As you reflect on yourself and the ways in which you seek to obey God, at what places in your life do you most need the gift of the Holy Spirit to bring change and growth in obedience and service to the Lord?

4

PRIVATE LIVES AND
PUBLIC LIVES

Matthew 6:1–18

In this chapter, we turn to the second setting in which Jesus taught the Lord's Prayer. On this occasion, the prayer comes in the middle of one of Jesus' best-known public discourses—the section of Matthew that we refer to as the Sermon on the Mount. In his introduction to the Lord's Prayer, Jesus says:

> And when you pray, do not heap up empty phrases as the Gentiles do, for they think that they will be heard for their many words. Do not be like them, for your Father knows what you need before you ask him. Pray then like this:
> "Our Father in heaven, hallowed be your name."
> (Matt. 6:5–9)

When Jesus teaches the Lord's Prayer on this occasion, the prayer comes in the context of a wider discussion about the nature of prayer, giving, and fasting—those things that might be described as our personal acts of devotion.

This subject of personal devotion is a very challenging one for all Christian believers to reflect on and to practice. Even more than usual, I feel inadequate in addressing this matter of our personal acts of devotion. I am no prayer warrior, no champion faster, no great giver, as God knows, but feel very much like the person who came to Jesus and said: "Lord, I believe; help my unbelief!" (Mark 9:24), or like the woman who so longed to be made whole that she wanted to touch just the hem of Jesus' robe that she might be healed of her sickness (Luke 8:44). So this is my prayer as I write: "Lord, help me!"

Even though I feel so unqualified to write about personal devotion to the Lord, my comfort, in attempting to reflect on this subject, is that I know I am not alone in my awareness of insufficiency. I do not think I have ever met a true Christian who can say: "I am really good at praying, at fasting, and at giving!" Even to write down such a claim makes it appear arrogant and absurd.

Yet Jesus, as he teaches on personal devotion, assumes that we all give, that we all pray, and that we all fast. He introduces each of these subjects by saying quite simply and directly: "When you give to the needy . . ."; "And when you pray . . ."; "And when you fast . . ." (Matt. 6:2, 5, 7, 16).

ACTS OF RIGHTEOUSNESS

Beware of practicing your righteousness before other people in order to be seen by them, for then you will have no reward from your Father who is in heaven.

Thus, when you give to the needy, sound no trumpet before you, as the hypocrites do in the synagogues and in the streets, that they may be praised by others. (Matt. 6:1–2a)

As he introduces the subject of our personal devotion to the Lord, Jesus speaks about "acts of righteousness" (NIV) or "practicing your righteousness" (ESV) (Matt. 6:1). Prayer, fasting, and giving are indeed a part of genuine righteousness when they are practiced in a manner that pleases the Lord. It is clear, however, that Jesus is addressing the wrong ways in which we often think about giving, praying, and fasting, as well as the right ways in which we ought to think about these things.

As we reflect on these words of Jesus, we need to think about what the Lord desires to see in us. The Word teaches us that the Lord delights to receive true righteousness from us—not a surface appearance of righteousness, but a righteousness rising from deep within us. He longs for us to love him with our whole being and to love with genuine love the people around us. He is eager for us to be just, merciful, and generous in all our dealings with others, and he yearns for us to offer ourselves to him, every day, without reservation and with glad hearts. His desire is that we hold nothing back from him.

Instead of this true devotion from the heart, we are mostly satisfied with somewhat superficial displays of our Christian commitment. We perform "acts of righteousness," "religious duties," or "devotions" and offer them to God, to prove to him, to others, and perhaps even to ourselves that we are serious, devout, holy-minded, good Christians. Without being aware of it, we become like the Pharisee (Luke 18:9–14) whose prayer was a list of his "acts of righteousness."

When this Pharisee prayed, he set out an impressive record of his practices of righteousness to the Lord. He thought of himself as a giver—"I give tithes of all that I get" (v. 12). He considered himself a faster—"I fast," he said, "twice a week" (v. 12). He imagined himself a praying man—there he was, praying in the temple to prove it. No doubt he attended the synagogue worship services as often as they were held, not only on the Sabbath but also on market days such as Tuesday and Thursday—when synagogue services were also held for people coming into town from the countryside.

SELF-FOCUSED DEVOTION

But if we think about giving, praying, and fasting as that Pharisee did, our focus is not truly on God at all; rather, our focus is on ourselves. Like the Pharisee, we give, and yet we are really giving to prove something about ourselves. We are not giving to the Lord out of love for him, nor are we giving to others because we care about them in any deep way. We fast, and yet we are fasting to show ourselves how devout we are, rather than because we know that we need the Lord. We pray, and yet we are praying to demonstrate to ourselves how prayerful we are. In fact, we are just like the Pharisee, of whom Jesus said that "he prayed about himself" (Luke 18:11 NIV).

DEVOTION TO IMPRESS GOD

If our focus is on ourselves rather than on the Lord, then we become proud of our giving, of our fasting, and of our praying, just as the Pharisee did. Where will such pride lead? Soon we begin to imagine that our giving, fasting, and praying is building up credit for ourselves before God. That was clearly the attitude of the Pharisee of whom

Jesus spoke in his parable, for the man was thanking God that he was not like other people—because, unlike such sinners, he could point the Lord to his record of devotion: his giving, fasting, and praying. This man clearly believed that God was indebted to him because he was so devout. It is easy for all of us to begin to think like this—that God will be indebted to us because we give and pray and fast. Or we might suppose that we will ensure that God will not punish us, but rather will overlook our failures and sins, because we have given so much, or have prayed so faithfully, so lengthily, and so often, or have fasted so earnestly and so regularly.

One of the most amusing yet sad illustrations of such "acts of devotion" was imposed by a local pastor on a parishioner who, by his careless driving, had caused an accident that injured a friend of mine, one of our seminary students. In confession to his pastor, the man acknowledged that he had injured someone by not looking carefully enough when he drove across a busy road, and that he had hit another person's car head on. His pastor imposed on him the penance of having to say the Lord's Prayer a specific number of times each day for a month.

Our student (we will call him "Fred" for this story) made the effort to get to know the man who had caused the accident. In one of their conversations over coffee together, it came out that Fred was an assistant pastor. When the man reported this to his pastor, the penance was doubled! The "sinner" was required to say twice as many "Our Fathers" for hitting a pastor than if he had hit a less "holy" man.

We hear this example and we laugh, as well as experience distress over such a misuse of the Lord's Prayer. We realize, in an obvious case like this, that the praying of the

Lord's Prayer has been turned into a religious duty that is being offered to God to increase his goodwill toward us by the number of times we repeat the words of the prayer. Yet while it is easy to make fun of such an example, the far sadder truth is that, even without being aware of it, all of us very easily begin to think like this about our praying, about our giving, and about our fasting.

DEVOTION TO IMPRESS OTHERS

From these kinds of attempts to impress God, or to try to earn credit with him, there is only a short distance to showing off our devotion to impress others. If our focus is on doing "acts of righteousness" to please God, to earn his favor or to avoid his displeasure, and to feel better about our own spirituality, then we will soon be doing these things for the approval of others. We give to the needy, and we make sure that someone knows about it, and we hope the someone who knows will spread the word of our generosity so that others will hear about it, too, and say: "Did you know how generous Jerram is?"

Like the hypocrites of whom Jesus speaks, we send someone ahead of us as we parade down the street to announce our giving with "trumpets." Anyone who doubts that Jesus had a sense of humor need only think about the ludicrousness of the picture that his words conjure up before our eyes! But I am sure that we could all cite examples, both from the general society around us and from within the church, of people we have seen giving with a desire to impress others. The far sadder truth, however, is that we all know we have this longing for approval in ourselves as well. It is very difficult to give without wanting someone else to know about it.

In like manner, we pray so that others will see us praying, just as the hypocrites prayed standing in the front of the synagogue, at its entrance, or on the street corners.

> And when you pray, you must not be like the hypocrites. For they love to stand and pray in the synagogues and at the street corners, that they may be seen by others. (Matt. 6:5)

Jesus addresses several prayer practices that he considers "paraded acts of righteousness" rather than genuine devotion. In his day the synagogues were often built on a high place in the city or at a street corner. Jesus imagines a hypocrite standing at the synagogue door where the maximum number of people can see him from as many directions as possible. In addition, the man is holding up other worshipers as he prays a long prayer in the doorway of the synagogue—all to show off his spirituality. If a line formed of people waiting to come in for worship, everyone would know how devoted he was in his prayer life, how zealous to worship the Lord. Again, the picture Jesus paints for us is amusing and is intended to demonstrate the self-centered folly of this practice—but the truth is that we see many such displays of devotion in our churches, and sometimes we make such displays ourselves.

In the synagogue services in Jesus' day, the prayer time was made up of eighteen brief prayers: "the eighteen benedictions." The first three and the last three of these were written out and were repeated at each service. The middle twelve were made up by the person chosen to lead prayers that week. Jesus is criticizing those who pray twelve long prayers in the synagogue services to parade their impressive gift of prayer.

Again, we can all list examples of people whom we suspect of praying long prayers to impress others with their fervor and devotion. But again, the far sadder truth is that many of us must acknowledge that we struggle with this temptation, too—some of us by praying ostentatiously, loudly, or lengthily; others of us by refusing to pray publicly, perhaps because we are afraid that others will see the poverty of our spirituality and our inability to pray well.

I remember a well-known Christian leader, whom I greatly admire, making the mistake of saying in a meeting that when he asked people to pray, he could gauge the status of their relationship with the Lord. He was not intending to intimidate, nor was he really suggesting that prayer was an infallible pointer to the spiritual state of others' hearts—he was simply commenting that we learn about their inner life from their prayers. Yet the impact of his words was to make many of the younger staff members far too self-aware when they had to pray in public. Some of us would try to hide behind one another so that he wouldn't ask us to pray! We were all acutely aware of the inadequate nature of our prayer lives, and we did not want our immaturity exposed in public.

> And when you fast, do not look gloomy like the hypo-crites, for they disfigure their faces that their fasting may be seen by others. (Matt. 6:16)

When he addresses the subject of fasting, once again Jesus makes fun of the desire of some to impress those around them by their eagerness to serve the Lord in a personally taxing manner—and obviously so, for others to see and to praise. We fast, and like the hypocrites, we make sure that others know we are fasting. We try to appear gloomy and disfigure our faces, as Jesus says (again with a touch of humor). We make ourselves look somber and serious-minded, making faces or grasping our stomachs to demonstrate how hungry we are. Or we might even say to someone: "I had such a great time of prayer and fasting, but boy, is my stomach grumbling!" "I always enjoy times of fasting—but I find that I get a little faint after the first seven or eight hours!" We all have many ways of showing off like this, and Jesus desires to expose them all.

Jesus' words enable us to see how foolish we can be. Indeed, it can be truly helpful to learn to laugh at ourselves. I do not mean that it is wise or beneficial to become cynical about my own heart or my own temptations to hypocrisy, for cynicism is destructive. The Lord knows our weaknesses completely and, thankfully, he is never cynical about us. It is wise and it is helpful, however, to be able to laugh at ourselves and to learn not to take ourselves so seriously. Jesus' humor cuts through our pride, our pomposity, and our parading of our piety.

But another issue is important. These words of Jesus— about "acts of devotion" to impress ourselves, to impress God, and to impress others—get us to the very heart of why we all struggle with prayer and why, so often, we find some teaching on prayer discouraging rather than encouraging. I believe that whenever teaching on prayer suggests that by sustained application of particular disciplines we can improve the quality and fervor of our devotional lives, several problems soon begin to surface.

If we actually succeed in observing the disciplines, and so increase the time, frequency, and passion of our prayers, there is the danger of spiritual pride. We easily begin to believe that we know God better, that our relationship with him is becoming deeper, and perhaps even that he loves us more because we are doing well at our devotions.

Or if, on the other hand, we find ourselves failing at the disciplines, we become miserable. We are exposed in our spiritual inadequacy. We become confused and depressed about the poor state of our devotional lives. We are tempted to believe that God loves us less because of our weak prayer lives. Whenever there is a public element to our praying, our giving, and our fasting, then these difficulties are increased. When we practice our devotion in public, our sense of our spiritual strength (or our spiritual weakness) is magnified because we know that we are on display and that we will be judged by others.

THE PROBLEM OF LEADERSHIP

This problem of turning giving, praying, and fasting into public acts for the approval of others, or into a display of our spirituality, is a particular challenge for anyone in a position of church leadership. I teach at a seminary, working with colleagues and students. All of us are involved with public ministry or are in training for such lifelong work. We all either are or will be in leadership in a church or in some other ministry. We seek to serve God and his people. In all that we do at the seminary, we are preparing ourselves in our times together, so that we might be a blessing to our families, to our friends, to fellow believers, and to people who do not yet know the Lord. This is true for all believers: whether at a seminary or in our churches, together we are working at being "public" Christians.

PUBLIC PRAYING

We are preparing ourselves for a lifetime of public praying. Indeed, all of us wrestle with this issue, not only those who are called to be pastors and teachers in the churches, or missionaries, or leaders in ministries. All through our lives we are going to be teaching others to pray. This is true for every Christian mother or father, for we have a responsibility to teach our children to pray, and this requires us to model praying for them. Many of us will be required to pray publicly when we are helping with a Sunday school class or Bible study, even if we have never thought of ourselves as leaders. Whenever any one of us is involved in helping a non-Christian come to faith in Jesus, we will have occasion to pray with and for that person.

Such "public praying" is a part of parenthood, and a part of the life of almost all growing Christians. Public prayer is an essential part of any kind of leadership or ministry among God's people. This means, of course, that we should want to learn to be a helpful and encouraging example of prayer, whether for our own children or for anyone else we seek to serve. A dear friend of mine is called the "designated pray-er" by the rest of the staff in his real estate office. He is one of the few committed Christians there, and so the others always turn to him and say "Joe, pray for us!" if they need a pleasant day for their work or for an office picnic, or if someone is sick.

Of course, Joe does not boast about his praying, but he is open and vocal about his Christian faith. He is also a man who has integrity at work, and he is kind, gracious, thoughtful, and respectful to everyone. The consequence is that he is regarded by everyone with deep affection and with genuine admiration, and his fellow workers see him as a man of prayer. Whenever a problem or need arises, they will look to him and tell him about it, to make sure that he will pray. Many of you who are reading this will have had the same experience in your extended families and in other settings—whenever a prayer is to be said at a meal, or at some significant family or social occasion, you will be the one who is asked to pray. You will become the "designated pray-er" in your family, in your workplace, and among your friends—especially if you are the only known Christian believer.

PUBLIC FASTING

All through our lives we are going to be teaching others to fast, and also leading them in times of fasting. Again, we will be publicly seeking to set an example. We will be giving people guidelines—practical helps and tips so that they may be able to fast well. We might say, for example: "I find that such-and-such a practice is helpful," or "Make sure you have water to drink, if you are praying and taking a long walk," or "If you have any medical problems, it would be wise to consult a doctor before you take on any extended time of fasting."

For almost twenty years my wife, Vicki, and I worked in L'Abri Fellowship, the ministry started by Francis and Edith Schaeffer in the Swiss Alps, and now having seven or eight branches around the world. In L'Abri we had regular days of fasting and prayer. The Schaeffers had been greatly influenced by the ministry and writing of Amy Carmichael, who founded the wonderful work of Dohnavur in southern India. Carmichael had written about times of prayer and fasting, so it was quite natural to read the helpful suggestions in her works. Consequently, our days of fasting and prayer were very much shaped by Carmichael's "public" reflections and practices—and this is a right and good thing.

PUBLIC GIVING

All through our lives we are going to be teaching about giving—giving of our finances, of our time, of our energy, of our homes in hospitality—and again, this is public in a sense. It is certainly so for our children. We must teach them to be generous, both by precept and by example. The church treasurer or deacons' board usually has a record of how much people give. These records are needed for tax purposes; taxes are a matter of public record, so anyone can check on what someone claims to have given to charity. People see how we give of our time and our energy and whether our homes are open to others. One cannot practice hospitality with absolute secrecy!

The life of any leader at any level in the life of the church is an open book for others to read and evaluate the reality of commitment in our lives. This is true of any Christian, whether we are "chiefs of thousands, of hundreds, of fifties, and of tens" (Ex. 18:17–23), or whether we influence one or two—our own children or a friend who is a new convert. All of us who have children must be aware that our children observe whether our "religious" words outside and inside the home and our teaching God's truth to them are matched by the way we live. They see whether our prayers and our lives are marching in step, or whether in fact there is a radical disjunction between the two. They hear us read passages of Scripture about generosity and giving; they hear us telling them how a Christian should give. They notice whether we are in fact generous or whether, instead, we spend almost all we have on our own personal and family needs and wants.

THE NEED FOR MODELS

This "public reality" of our "acts of righteousness" is an essential part of the Christian life, no matter how challenging it is for us, because there is indeed a need for models. In the situations that I have been describing, it is right and good that we are public Christians. It is right and good that our children, for example, hear us praying, for then our prayers can become an encouragement and an example for them as they themselves learn to pray. This is true for every new Christian, too—public models of prayer are necessary for them.

And this is true for us all—we all need examples. In God's Word, the prayers of Moses, of Hannah, of David, of Mary, and of Jesus himself are an encouragement and a pattern for us as we learn to pray. The whole church throughout her history has seen the book of Psalms as the private prayer book of the believer and also as the public worship manual of the people of God.

As it is with our prayers, so it is with our giving and our fasting. This is necessary and good simply because all believers learn and need to learn from the example of others. The writer of Hebrews urges us to remember the outcome of our leaders' way of life, and to imitate their faith (Heb. 13:7). The apostle Paul calls us to imitate him as he imitates Christ (1 Cor. 11:1). As was mentioned earlier, all of us are called to be examples for our children and for our fellow Christians to imitate. We do not have to blow a trumpet and announce what we are doing. People will know—unless we are indeed complete hypocrites who only tell others to pray, to give, and to fast, but never do these things ourselves! That, unhappily, is possible, too!

Whether, then, we are leaders of God's people or not, we will be public Christians to some degree or other. We cannot avoid people's seeing and hearing us pray, give, or fast, and so we gain respect, often more respect than we can properly handle. This respect makes our lives that much more challenging.

JESUS' QUESTION

> When you pray, you must not be like the hypocrites.
> For they love to stand and pray . . . , that they may be
> seen by others. Truly, I say to you, they have received
> their reward. (Matt. 6:5)

The question that Jesus sets before each one of us is this: "Is this public praying, giving, and fasting all you do?" If this is the case, then it is clear that our praying, giving, and fasting are simply "acts of righteousness" to gain credit with God, to feel better about ourselves, and to earn the approval and praise of others.

To behave in such a manner would be like a man or a woman who is kind and courteous to his or her spouse only in public—but who, in the privacy of the home, is rude, selfish, demanding, and maybe even abusive. Sadly, this is sometimes the truth. We all know such families—what is seen in public, the appearance of a happy family life, is all there is, and it is only a hypocritical shell.

In the same way, it is possible for professed believers in Christ to excel at seeming to be shining examples in front of others. If we are only "public" Christians, however, only models on show in a window display of spirituality, then the praise and approval of others is all that we will receive. Jesus makes this very clear: the approval of others will be our only reward.

God desires something more from us. He does not want from us a list of our religious accomplishments or acts of devotion. He wants love from us. He wants us!

SECRET GIVING

God desires us to give secretly so that no one else knows, so that there may be no church records, no tax receipts, but just generous impulses for some of what we give (so that we ourselves may not even know exactly how much we have given). The Lord delights in anonymous giving. At the seminary where I teach, one of the student apartment buildings was given anonymously, to honor the ministry of Francis and Edith Schaeffer. I tried to find out who had given the gift so that I could thank the person on behalf of Edith Schaeffer (with whom my wife and I had worked in the ministry of L'Abri for many years). I assured the office that I would not publicize the name or even tell Edith. But the instructions were clear—this gift was to be a complete secret. No one was to know. I was deeply moved by this, and much more importantly, so is the Lord. He wants us to be so touched by his love for us that we give cheerfully, without counting the cost; that we give impulsively, simply because we see need; and that we give, most of all, because our own needs have been so wonderfully met by Christ.

Here I will give the example of my father-in-law. While I was in theological seminary in the late 1960s, my wife and I would drive from St. Louis to central California each summer, and I would help out on the family farm. Dear Dad had a small farm in the San Joaquin Valley, and he grew tree fruit such as peaches, nectarines, plums, and persimmons, and he also grew some grapes and kiwis. In the summer of 1969 we were staying with Mom and Dad, enjoying their wonderful hospitality as we did so many times, and I was helping to pick and pack watermelons.

One day I was walking back to the house through the fields for lunch, and I came across Dad kneeling in his orchards, offering the firstfruits of his young peach trees to the Lord. When a peach tree is three or four years old, it will bear its firstfruits—it will have four or five large, beautiful peaches, some of the finest fruit that the tree will ever bear.

Dad was kneeling there, holding up a peach in each hand, and saying: "Lord, these peaches are yours. These trees are yours and all the fruit they will ever bear. This orchard is yours. My farm is yours. I am yours. Thank you for your love to me in Jesus. Help me to serve you in all I do."

Dad loved to read the Scriptures, and as he read in the books of Moses, he had decided for himself that he wanted to put into practice some of the various offerings and services in the Old Testament law that were required of the people of Israel. He thus regularly held this service of firstfruits just between himself and the Lord. He never told anyone about it (not even his own family)—it was a private matter between himself and the Lord.

I waited till he had finished his prayer and risen from his knees. He was a bit embarrassed to find me watching and listening to what he had thought was just between him and the Lord. I asked him about it, and he explained that he did this every time any of his trees started bearing their firstfruits. The Lord had taught Moses to command the people to bring the best of their firstfruits to the house of the Lord and offer them to him, so that is what he was doing.

The consequences of this little ceremony were remarkable. First, it impacted Dad's attitude toward his employees and anyone with whom he did business. He did not ask about his "bottom line" when he was thinking about paying the men who worked on his farm. Rather, he asked what would be pleasing to the Lord, what was just, merciful, and fair. In the last couple of years of Dad's life, a Latino man came by the house to thank him—he had worked for Dad many years ago. He said: "Every summer I would come up from Mexico and I would make a beeline for your farm. You treated us so much better than the other farmers. You did not pay minimum wage or the going rate. You paid us far more. You often ate lunch with us. You brought us treats at break time. You asked about our families. Working for you changed my whole life and the way I have raised my own sons. I should have come back to thank you before." By this time in his dementia, Dad did not understand what he was saying—but the rest of the family did!

At Dad's memorial service, we heard testimony that he had paid people more than they were worth, and some would express that fact to Dad when he handed them their checks. Even when others, including relatives, took advantage of his integrity and generosity, Dad never held it against them, but continued to treat them as well as everyone else—with the same kindness and mercy that he always showed to people. I am sure that almost everyone who knew him, worked with him, or did any business with him in any setting could tell numerous stories about this aspect of his commitment to treat people with justice and mercy.

Second, when Dad gave, he gave generously without thinking about precisely how much he could afford. In many years, although he was not a wealthy man, he gave away more than 50 percent of his income. He gave to his church, to ministries, and to many individuals. He did not keep careful records of all his giving, though of course he received tax-deductible receipts for the more regular gifts. He was once audited by the Internal Revenue Service for giving away too much of his income. The IRS sent him a personal letter of commendation, both for the honesty and clearness of his bookkeeping and also for his extraordinary generosity. The IRS informed him, however, that he could not give so much and claim it all as tax-deductible. He was giving over the limit.

Of course, that did not cause him to give less. He had had no idea that there was a "limit" to what one could give—he carried on giving just as generously, but was careful to claim only the portion of his giving that was within the legal limit.

SECRET FASTING

Just as the Lord desires that we give secretly, he also wants us to fast privately, so that only God knows that we are fasting. He longs to have us say to him: "Lord, I need you more than food. I long to be genuinely righteous. So, Lord, please feed me with your life, with your Spirit. Lord, make me like your Son!" We all need to build times into our lives when we go without a meal or two, without letting anyone but the Lord know about our fast. Situations of personal need, or personal thanksgiving, or particular struggles we are having with sin, or times of major decision-making—these are ideal times for such private fasting.

SECRET PRAYING

In addition to secret giving and secret fasting, Jesus calls us to times of secret praying. We are to pray privately, so that we can tell the Lord that we love him and need him—just between him and me. He wants to know that we recognize our need for his mercy and his love to enable us to be kind and generous. He wants to know that we acknowledge our need for him to root out the selfishness and pride in our hearts, for we can never do this completely by ourselves. He wants to know that we are aware of our need for his help even in our praying—that we are prepared to come to him privately and say: "Lord, teach me to pray!" In private, just with him, it is much easier to stop pretending that we are spiritual and eloquent in our prayers. The Lord desires us to be like Jesus, who woke up every morning eager to learn from his Father (Isa. 50:4–5).

He is eager to hear us tell him that we are full of gladness and joy because of the beauty of spring, because of the glory of a fall day, or because of the splendor of a night sky. He wants praise to burst out in our prayers and songs to overflow from our hearts (prayers and songs that no one hears but him) because we are so pleased to be loved and forgiven by him. He wants us to be so full of wonder and delight that we pray secretly without the knowledge of others in our household. He wants us to pray when we are in bed lying awake, when we are washing the dishes, when we are in the yard weeding the flowers, when we are driving our cars, when we are working around the house.

He simply wants me to express my love for him and my need for him, and he wants me to do this secretly—just him and me together.

This is the giving, this is the fasting, and this is the praying that God delights in. He sees in secret and he rewards in full by pouring his Spirit richly into our hearts and lives, by lavishing us with his love, and by making us into the likeness of his Son.

This teaching of Jesus on prayer is so simple and so encouraging! From it we learn both of the eagerness of God to listen and help us and also of the ease and directness with which we can come to our loving Father with our prayers.

Questions for Reflection and Discussion

1. In what contexts do you pray before others?

2. Do you struggle with the tension of needing to be an example of prayer to others, and yet feeling that you are not much good at praying in private?

3. Do you find that seeking to be disciplined in your devotional life can very easily lead to legalism, pride, or despondency?

4. In what inappropriate ways do you think about your relationship with the Lord and about your spiritual maturity? What are the appropriate ways, and how will you begin to implement them?

5. When do you think fasting would be most appropriate in your own personal life?

6. When do you think fasting might be appropriate in the life of your church?

7. Have you found yourself wanting others to know about your giving? How might you resolve this problem?

8. How does the thought that God simply wants you—that he longs to have you praising him and praying to him privately, just you and God alone together—help you to grasp the thrust of Jesus' words in Matthew 6?

5

PERSEVERANCE IN PRAYER

Luke 18:1–8

The discussion of God's desire that our devotion be private—primarily a matter between each of us personally and the Lord—leads us naturally to the matter of perseverance in prayer. Jesus, in his teaching on prayer recorded in Luke chapter 18, encourages us to persevere in prayer. Again, this matter of perseverance is something that we all find very difficult. Jesus, of course, is aware of how easily we lose heart, and how quickly we stop praying. That is why he gives us this particular teaching, as he makes clear when he introduces his parable.

The text begins: "He told them a parable to the effect that they ought always to pray and not lose heart" (Luke 18:1). Jesus then tells his parable and finishes with a further comment:

> "In a certain city there was a judge who neither feared God nor respected man. And there was a widow in that city who kept coming to him and saying, 'Give me

justice against my adversary.' For a while he refused, but afterward he said to himself, 'Though I neither fear God nor respect man, yet because this widow keeps bothering me, I will give her justice, so that she will not beat me down by her continual coming.'" And the Lord said, "Hear what the unrighteous judge says. And will not God give justice to his elect, who cry to him day and night? Will he delay long over them? I tell you, he will give justice to them speedily. Nevertheless, when the Son of Man comes, will he find faith on earth?" (Luke 18:2–8)

As we read this parable, we should carefully note that the story's purpose is to make a point through stark contrast. The story is about a persistent widow and an unjust judge. The judge finally gives in and hears the cries of the widow for justice because he is fed up with her constant bothering of him. He is not a good man. He does not fear God, nor does he respect other human persons—and he even knows this about himself! He is not committed to hearing those who bring their cases to him, and he is not concerned for justice. He pays attention to this woman only because he hopes that his listening to her plea will finally shut her up! The point of the parable is that this judge is totally unlike God—and yet even such a man can be worn down with persistence.

JUSTICE FOR THE PEOPLE OF GOD

God, says Jesus, is completely different from this unjust judge. The judge thinks of people's complaints and cries for justice as bothersome interruptions, whereas God delights in listening to his beloved people. The judge listens to the widow only because he does not want to have to keep hearing her demands for his mediation in her case; God, in contrast, does not need to be worn down by our constant requests. The unjust judge has to be manipulated by the widow. We are not, by our prayers, twisting God's arm; nor are we causing him to stop being reluctant to listen to us. The judge has no interest in listening to those who come before him. God gladly hears his chosen people as they cry out to him day and night. The judge wants to keep putting off the time for hearing those who have experienced unjust treatment. God is eager to see that people get justice, and that they get it quickly.

We may summarize Jesus' teaching in this way: we are praying to a God who hears us gladly; when we come to him with our troubles, we can be sure that he will hear us with immediate sympathy; we are promised that our heavenly Father has the will and the power to act quickly on behalf of his beloved people.

The context of Jesus' words teaches us about God's concern to make sure that his people receive justice in a world that is full of injustice. Yet this teaching raises all sorts of questions for us. We can say, first: "Yes, we know that God often answers prayers for justice for our fellow believers."

The Bible contains many examples. We can see such answers in the lives of believers such as David, Ruth, and Hannah. God answers their prayers for justice and shows mercy to them in their troubles.

We can also point to many examples in recent history. Think of the fall of the Communist governments of eastern and central Europe and the former Soviet Union. These were, just a few years ago, countries where Christians were persecuted by their governments and by many unjust laws. Conditions for believers in the former Communist world have now dramatically changed.

God heard the multitude of prayers that arose to him from believers all over the world for the persecuted churches of much of the Communist-dominated world. Today in many of those nations, Christians enjoy far greater freedom to practice and to share their faith than they did just two decades ago. The events that took place in East Germany, the Czech Republic, and Romania to bring about the end of the former regimes prompted special times of prayer and thanksgiving in churches around the world.

We can also think of the very recent example of another former Soviet-bloc country. When I was teaching a seminary class there several years ago, despite the fall of Communism the country was still ruled by a corrupt and thoroughly unjust government, a government controlled by the Mafia, rather than by Communist Party hard-liners (in fact, the Mafia were the former Communist Party hard-liners). The peaceful revolution that took place a year later was an extraordinary answer to the prayers of great numbers of Christians, both there and elsewhere. Instead of the difficulties and persecution that Christians were still experiencing under the previous regime, the new government appointed a highly respected Christian pastor to head up what had formerly been its secret police—one of the most corrupt and wicked organizations in the nation.

I could cite many such examples from different eras of church history, and many examples of individual believers having their prayers for justice answered. I am confident that as you read this, you can also think of personal illustrations from your own life or from the lives of family members or close friends.

WHAT ABOUT THOSE WHO ARE NOT DELIVERED FROM INJUSTICE?

Even though there are many such examples of wonderful deliverances from evil, we all know of Christians who continue to suffer terrible injustice. God does not always intervene to bring justice in this world in answer to the prayers of suffering Christians. Think, for example, of the martyrdom and enslavement of hundreds of thousands of believers in the Sudan over the past twenty years. What are we to make of these seemingly unanswered prayers, when Jesus speaks with such conviction and passion about God's answering them "speedily"?

Jesus gives the hint of an answer with his final comment: "Nevertheless, when the Son of Man comes, will he find faith on earth?" (Luke 18:8). These words allude to what Scripture teaches elsewhere about the need for believers to be ready to suffer, and the challenge not to lose faith in the face of such suffering. We must recognize that Scripture reminds us that Christians are defined as those "who follow the Lamb wherever he goes" (Rev. 14:4). All of us are called to deny ourselves, to take up our cross, and to follow Christ (Matt. 16:24).

This calling to follow Christ may very well mean that just like Christ, we Christians will not receive justice in this life. This was true for him even though he asked that he might be spared from his soon-coming cruel death. Jesus prayed with fervency: "My Father, if it be possible, let this cup pass from me" (Matt. 26:39). Yet Jesus did not have his prayer answered with immediate justice in this life. We are told that his prayer came from deep within his heart, for he had just told the disciples who were his dearest friends: "My soul is very sorrowful, even to death" (v. 38). Matthew tells us that Jesus persevered in this prayer and that, three times, he expressed his hope that he might not have to be crucified.

There is no doubt that the Father listened to Jesus gladly—he was perfect in thought, word, and deed. He had never displeased his Father in any way. We know that because of his desire to do whatever his Father wished, Jesus added this to his passionate words of longing that he would not have to endure the terrible suffering of the cross: "Nevertheless, not as I will, but as you will" (Matt. 26:39). We also know the outcome. Jesus was unjustly arrested, unjustly tried, unjustly found guilty, unjustly executed.

The same fate has come to many Christians throughout this age, from the time of Jesus' death and resurrection up until today, and these unjust deaths will continue to come to vast numbers of believers until Christ returns. In fact, there are more martyrs every year right now than there have been at any other point in the history of the church.

WERE JESUS' PRAYERS UNANSWERED?

Does this mean that God failed to answer the prayers for justice of his Son, Jesus, and the prayers of all these other Christians who have suffered unjust arrest, unjust trial, unjust imprisonment, and unjust death? Of course not! God answered Jesus' prayer for justice by raising him from the dead and, ultimately, by making him triumphant over all his enemies. In exactly the same way, God will answer the prayers for justice that every single believer makes by raising them from the dead and giving them ultimate victory over their enemies. Their future will be an eternal weight of glory beyond all comparison with their present sufferings.

Jesus did not waver in his trust of his heavenly Father— even though his prayers were not answered by the Father's sparing him from death on the cross. Rather, as Hebrews tells us, the Son learned obedience through what he suffered (Heb. 5:8). The question that Jesus poses for us is this: "Will we continue to trust our heavenly Father if he does not answer our prayers for speedy justice, but instead asks us to follow Christ in enduring injustice in this life? Will we endure till the end and be found to have faith despite the troubles we may be asked to undergo?"

OTHER KINDS OF TROUBLE

Am I suggesting, by this brief discussion of persecution and justice, that Jesus' teaching about perseverance in prayer can be applied only to the prayers for justice that are offered up by afflicted believers? Not at all! It is evident from Luke's introduction to the parable of the unjust judge that the words about persevering in prayer apply to every kind of trouble that we might experience in this world. Luke writes: "He told them a parable to the effect that they ought always to pray and not lose heart" (Luke 18:1). "Always" implies that Jesus is encouraging us to pray with confidence, no matter what our sorrows may be. In just the same way that God is committed to care for those enduring injustice, to hear their prayers gladly, and to answer them, even so he is committed to care for believers enduring all sorts of difficulties and to hear their prayers.

So whenever a dear friend or family member suffers, we are encouraged to cry out to God repeatedly. We become sick with longing to see them made well, to see their health restored, their troubles taken away, their unbelief turned to faith, their obstinate sin transformed into obedience. Such longing is right and good. Such persevering prayer is right and good. Failure to pray like this would demonstrate both a lack of faith and a lack of compassion on our part. It would show that we do not trust the Lord and that we do not truly care about anyone else's pain, troubles, sin, or lack of faith.

WHEN SHOULD WE STOP PRAYING SUCH PRAYERS?

I cannot answer this question, for Scripture gives us no rule. Our prayers for an unbeliever to turn to Christ, or for a straying fellow believer to repent of his or her sin and to become obedient to the Lord, should probably never cease as long as we have life and breath, for we know that God loves to save, and we know that his will is his people's growth in righteousness. Almost all Christians can give examples of family members and friends for whom many hundreds or even thousands of prayers have been offered up.

I was recently giving a series of lectures and sermons at the church where one of my seminary's graduates had been made the senior pastor. At the first teaching session, I noticed the presence of someone who seemed vaguely familiar to me, though I could not remember ever having met her. After the discussion time following the lecture, this person came and introduced herself to me. It turned out that I had known her father for many years and also one of her brothers. The father was one of the most godly, faithful people I have ever met. The brother was a cherished fellow elder in the denomination in which I served for many years. I had seen the family resemblance. This woman (now in her early sixties) told me how she had come to faith while she and the family were singing hymns around her father's deathbed—after decades of unbelief and wandering since turning away from God as a teenager. I am sure that she was a person for whom many thousands of prayers had been offered. I am also sure that praying with confidence was at times very difficult for that family and for others who loved them. Yet it is in just such situations that Jesus encourages us that we "ought always to pray and not lose heart" (Luke 18:1).

What about Prayers for the Sick and Similar Needs?

But this raises many more questions for us: "What about prayers for health and other such troubles in this world—how long should we keep on praying such prayers?" "What about persevering in prayer when someone we love is ill with a life-threatening disease, and we do not see him getting immediately well?" "Should we pray just once or twice, or is it good to keep on praying?"

We do not know the precise nature of the thorn in the flesh with which the apostle Paul wrestled—whether it was a physical malady or some other problem. In this particular case, Paul tells us that he prayed three times that his thorn in the flesh would be taken away. And then he stopped praying for the thorn's removal, but this was because he sensed God telling him that he would have to endure the thorn (2 Cor. 12:7–10). Paul had to be ready for a different kind of perseverance, and to be willing to persist in different prayers from those for healing. His calling was to pray for grace to endure the thorn, to pray for God's strength to sustain him in his ongoing weakness.

I struggle with acutely sensitive hearing because my inner ears were damaged after a bout with shingles. This illness usually causes deep depression, and in most cases the sufferer retires to live the life of a hermit to protect himself or herself from the constant assault of sound. I have come to a conclusion similar to that of the apostle Paul. I no longer pray for healing; rather, I pray for grace to endure the problem. My wife, on the other hand, will not give up praying for this affliction to be taken away, for she has a deep longing for my well-being and a passionate desire to be able to enjoy worship and music with me again—for with such hypersensitivity these pleasures are impossible for me.

Or let us take a much more serious example. We have a friend back in England who had a massive spinal injury more than thirty-five years ago. An outstanding gymnast, he was warming up for a display when he broke his neck doing a backward somersault. He was rushed to a special hospital with a spinal-injuries unit, and the medical personnel had to work very hard to save his life. That first night his heart stopped a dozen times, and they had to keep restarting it while they tried to repair a little of the damage. "What is so wonderful about this?" you ask. Certainly not the accident, or the fact that ever since that day our friend has been totally paralyzed from the neck down, confined to bed or to a wheelchair that he operates with his chin. He writes letters using a stick in his mouth to tap out the words on a computer keyboard.

There are many extraordinary things about his life. During one of the times his heart stopped that first night after his accident, he has a memory of the Lord speaking directly to him, and of his coming to trust in Christ. His faith is truly a vibrant faith. This man is one of the most cheerful people I have ever met, one of the least self-centered, without the slightest trace of self-pity. He still loves sports, and every Sunday at church, you would see a gaggle of little boys gathered around his wheelchair, chattering with him about the results of the soccer matches the day before, or about athletics or a cricket test match or the Tour de France or whatever other sporting event was currently taking place.

He served for perhaps twenty years as one of the deacons in our church. One of the most moving occasions for the whole church was when he married a young woman who had been a nurse at the special home for people with severe injuries and disabilities where he was a resident, for of course he is absolutely dependent on others to feed him, to bathe him, and to take care of all the other basic necessities of his life. My wife, Vicki, played the organ for his wedding, and remembering that day still brings tears to her eyes. At the time she could hardly see her music through her weeping. He and his wife were the leaders of the youth group for many years, and he would keep regular contact by e-mail with most of the young people when they left home and went off to college. He has become one of our dear longtime friends since I first met him in that residential care center. He still writes to us from time to time even though we have now been in the United States for more than eighteen years. In a great number of ways he is a shining example of what it means to be a person who loves God with his whole being and who loves his neighbor as himself.

Of course, all of us who know him long for the day when he will be able to walk and run again, when his body will obey his will once more—even far better than before. When this ultimate healing and restoration of his body happens, it will be, and he will be, something beautiful to behold. He will run and feel God's pleasure in the glory of having a functioning physical life.

But he knows, and his friends know, that this day will not come till he is with the Lord. I think all of us, including his parents and his wife, have not even considered praying for his physical healing for many, many years. Nor has he—yet he looks forward to the resurrection of his body and to everlasting life with his body performing far better than it did even when he was an outstanding gymnast.

Sometimes, as with our dear friend and the apostle Paul, we become convinced that God will not heal us in this life, or that he will not answer a particular request that we keep bringing to him—or rather, we become convinced that he will not answer our request in the way in which we hoped at first. In such a case we pray for strength in our weakness, just as Paul did. And because that is a prayer for spiritual help, we know with confidence that the Lord, who is the Father of all mercy and the God of all comfort, will certainly come to our aid. Here the words of encouragement from Luke chapter 11 apply: Jesus promises us that God always gives the Holy Spirit to those who ask him. So we must persevere with prayers for his help in our weakness until the day we die and go to be with him, or until the day of his return to make us new and to take us to be his own.

The same will be true of our prayers for one another to endure trials and to grow in faith and obedience. We prayed very often for Mom as she was taking care of Dad in his decline into dementia—and the Lord answered our prayers in the most remarkable way. After several years of caring for him, even though there had been very little communication for some time, she wrote to us that she thought that in some ways this was the happiest time of their life—in the end they were married for about sixty-eight years.

Much of the time, of course, she felt overwhelmed by the challenges that came to her every day, and particularly by the lack of communication with this man she had loved so faithfully for so long, and by his total dependence on her in every area—when she had depended on him for so many things for the greatest part of her life. My brother-in-law, a doctor, said, that if it were not for her care, Dad would have died long before; that toward the end, if (as happens in most such situations) he had undergone hospice care, he would almost certainly have been gone within a few weeks or months, instead of the years that he lived. But with such care as hers, he said, "All bets as to how long he will survive are off."

Again in this situation, while we prayed that the onset of dementia would be slowed, and we were all very thankful that Dad knew all the family, the Lord, and the Scriptures until the very end, yet I do not think that anyone prayed that he would be cured of dementia. We all prayed for his happiness through those final years; and we all prayed for Mom's strength and for constant grace, patience, and love for her. I expect that anyone with aging parents will understand exactly what I am trying to communicate. We all know that the last enemy, death, will not be destroyed until the return of Christ; and so we know that our prayers as death approaches must be for strength and grace, not for healing.

SURE CLAIMS OF CERTAIN HEALING OR DELIVERANCE?

This study of perseverance in prayer raises some very thought-provoking questions, in particular the difficult and even painful issue of whether we can ever claim with certainty that someone will be healed, or whether we can ever be sure that some other such prayer for deliverance from trouble, or from a situation of injustice, will definitely be answered in the way we so passionately desire.

We need to recognize that there are some basic problems in making such confident claims ourselves, or in encouraging others to make such claims as they pray.

PROBLEM ONE

The first problem is the claim of infallible certainty: "God has spoken to me and told me that this person will be healed, or that this prayer will be answered in this particular manner." Scripture alone has this kind of authority. We are not encouraged by God's Word to claim this kind of certainty for our own hopes, longings, or sense of God's leading. If we do make such claims, we are sure to cause even greater pain to those who suffer.

I will never forget a time when my wife had very serious back problems. At one point she was in bed for almost six months because she experienced severe pain in walking or any other movement as a result of two ruptured discs in her lower spine. Eventually she had two surgeries—the second one being a seven-hour operation in which the surgeon did a double fusion (from both back and front) of three of her vertebrae.

During this time—which was extraordinarily difficult for Vicki and for our family (with three young boys to care for)—several people came to me and insisted with claims of total certainty that they had prayed for her and that she would be healed. One young man, whom we hardly knew, had put his hand on her shoulder when he prayed for her and then said to me: "The Lord spoke to me as I prayed, and he promised that she would be healed and able to get up from her bed and walk within just a day or two."

While we are encouraged to pray with faith, and to lay hands on the sick, such claims of absolute certainty are not our prerogative in this life, and they only cause even greater sorrow.

PROBLEM TWO

A second problem is that such claims suggest that if we pray in just the right manner or with the right amount of trust, God will do what we ask. It is as if we were to say:

"God will have to do what I ask him to do because I have prayed in this particular way, or with this confidence." Such statements are insisting that if we pray in the appropriate manner and with enough faith, then we can walk by sight rather than by faith in this life; that we can know with complete certainty just what God will do for us because we prayed the right kind of prayer. This is the claim at the heart of many of the most popular books about prayer, and at the heart of much of the teaching on prayer that draws people to some of the teachers we see and hear in the media.

It is clear, however, that we ought never to make such claims, for this is not what the Lord promises us in this present time. This is one of the issues that Paul addresses in both 1 and 2 Corinthians, for this was the claim of the false teachers in the Corinthian church: "Already you have all you want! Already you have become rich! Without us you have become kings!" (1 Cor. 4:8). Paul rejects this teaching with great passion, and he reminds the Corinthians of the ongoing suffering in the lives of the apostles. He teaches that we are not now in the time when we can make claims that God will fix all our troubles. Rather, he reminds his readers of the reality of his life as an apostle: "We have become, and are still, like the scum of the world, the refuse of all things" (1 Cor. 4:13). Paul insists that the calling of Christians in this world is to take up the cross and follow the Lamb wherever he goes.

PROBLEM THREE

A third problem of such overly confident claims is that when disappointment comes, God is blamed as if he were the One at fault for not keeping his promises. But God has made no such promise to us of certain healing or certain success in this life. Indeed, he has told us precisely the opposite: that through much tribulation we must enter the kingdom of God. This was the teaching that Paul and Barnabas wanted to communicate to the new Christians in the churches that they had recently planted:

> They returned to Lystra and to Iconium and to Antioch, strengthening the souls of the disciples, encouraging them to continue in the faith, and saying that through many tribulations we must enter the kingdom of God. (Acts 14:21-22)

I remember meeting a family of five teenagers whose mother had recently died of cancer. The father had left years before. While the mother was in the hospital, the family's church elders had come in obedience to James's command (James 5:14) and anointed her with oil, laid hands on her, and prayed for her healing. The children appreciated this expression of faith and love.

But there were two serious errors. The pastor and elders promised her children that their mother would certainly be healed. When she died, less than two weeks later, the children were never visited again by the church leaders. They were left to deal with the funeral, and their great loss, with no help whatsoever from their church, their elders, or their pastor. These young people became angry with the Lord when the promises failed, and when the care of the church disappeared. Such anger is mistaken, of course, but is thoroughly understandable in such circumstances. These church leaders had not merely lied and failed, but misrepresented God himself.

PROBLEM FOUR

A fourth problem is that if God does not give the expected answer to this "guaranteed" kind of praying, then

88

the person who is not healed or otherwise delivered is blamed for lack of faith or for some hidden sin in his or her life. The teacher who has made false promises in such scenarios will never take the blame for the lack of healing, the collapse of a business, the continued experience of injustice at work, or whatever other problem he had promised that "the prayer of faith" would most assuredly set right. Rather, the person who continues to suffer or his or her family members are the ones blamed.

I have even seen believers disciplined by their pastors for not being healed, with the charge that their lack of healing was a result of their lack of faith. Or because a person had not believed the promise of certain healing the pastor had given, he or she was displaying a rebellious and disobedient spirit. I remember a woman who had ankylotic spondylitis of the spine. This is an appalling disease that causes the spine to become progressively more curved and rigid until the sufferer is bent almost double and is in severe and constant pain. Her pastor and his fellow leaders prayed over her and assured her that she had been healed. When she continued to worsen and her spine did not straighten and her pain became more severe, rather than receiving comfort from the leaders, she was thrown out of her church as a person with an unbelieving, embittered, and rebellious disposition.

Returning to the example of my wife's enduring severe back pain, so much so that she was bedridden for several months: along with much love and support from our own congregation, family, and friends, we received much criticism over her not being healed and because our doctors eventually decided that she needed extensive surgery. Some who came and claimed that Vicki was definitely healed after they had prayed for her blamed her, or me, when she continued to endure debilitating pain. They insisted that there was obviously secret sin in her life. Or I had ruined their prayer of faith by my lack of faith. One woman wrote me a fifteen-page letter saying that God had revealed to her that there was some terrible sin hidden away in my life, and that God was punishing my wife for my sin.

This, of course, was the view of Job's "comforters," who thought that continued suffering is always a sign of unconfessed sin. To them and those like them, there must be a direct and obvious correlation between our faith and obedience on the one hand and our health and prosperity on the other. Their conviction was that God balances the books perfectly in this life. Consequently, continued suffering is always a sign of unbelief and disobedience. Repentance and faith will necessarily fix the problem. This was also the view of the Pharisees, who assumed that the man born blind was being punished either for his own sins or for the sins of his parents (see John 9:13–34 for the lengthy exploration of this notion when Jesus heals the man).

Job's comforters were wrong. The Pharisees were wrong. My comforters, or rather my accusers, were wrong. Of course, my faith was not complete, nor was I perfectly righteous at that time in my life; neither was my wife without sin. The truth is that none of us are ever perfect in our faith and obedience in this life. Perfection must wait for the future life when we will be fully like Christ. In all our imperfections, however, the last thing any of us needs when we are suffering is comforters who claim to know God's will for us perfectly, and who blame us for our own pain. The Scripture forbids us to have such pretensions about perfect knowledge. This means that it is profoundly unbiblical, and certainly unchristian, to insist that we can know exactly what is happening in another sufferer's life. It is not our place to think that we can accuse one who is suffering of being guilty of secret sin or lack of faith if the person is not delivered from his or her trouble.

Such arrogant presumption is not countenanced by God's Word. In addition, these confident assertions of claiming to know why someone is sick and what God has done, is doing, and will do in someone's life are no substitute for the time-consuming care, the costly compassion, and the "weeping with those who weep" that the Scriptures ask of us. Instead, these blithe statements of ungodly presumption, which pretend spiritual discernment, are vain attempts to seek to heal people's wounds lightly and to cry, "Peace, peace," when there is no peace. Such an approach to the wounded makes it harder for them to cling to Jesus' encouragement "always to pray and not lose heart" (Luke 18:1). God forbid that we should add to people's sorrows rather than bear their burdens and so fulfill the law of Christ.

Questions for Reflection and Discussion

1. Have you (like many of us at times) thought of perseverance in prayer negatively, as if the Lord really were an unjust judge whom you must keep bothering to make sure that he will hear your prayers and answer you?

2. How should we think about perseverance in a positive way? What examples from your own life can you give of times or situations when you have had to persevere in praying for yourself or someone else many times, even for many years?

3. As you think back on the years you have been a Christian, what has it meant for you to deny yourself, take up your cross, and follow Jesus (Matt. 16:24)? What has it meant for you to be prepared to "follow the Lamb wherever he goes" (Rev. 14:4)?

4. How have you yourself dealt with the teaching that if we have enough faith, or that if we pray in just the right way, the Lord will do anything that we ask him: that he will always heal us from sickness, will always prosper us financially, and so on?

5. Have you tried to talk to fellow believers who insist that the Lord's call to deny ourselves, take up our cross, and follow him does not apply to issues of physical suffering, except for situations when we are being directly persecuted for our faith? Earlier I referred to Hebrews chapter 11, which tells us that some of those who live by faith may be miraculously delivered, and that others who live by faith are miraculously helped to endure unspeakable suffering. To what other Scriptures might you appeal to defend the view that your calling might well be to endure very difficult life situations?

6

Prayer, Fasting, and Discipline in Prayer

Matthew 6:5–6, 16–18;
Luke 5:12–16; 6:12–16

A t this time in my life, I teach at Covenant Theological Seminary in St. Louis, Missouri. The seminary community tries to schedule fairly regular days of prayer and fasting. Earlier in our lives, my wife and I worked with L'Abri Fellowship for almost twenty years. In addition, I served as a pastor in a church. From time to time, these ministries would have both regular and especially called days of prayer and fasting.

Francis and Edith Schaeffer, the founders of L'Abri, were greatly influenced by Amy Carmichael, who had begun a ministry, Dohnavur Fellowship in southern India, over a hundred years ago. Carmichael wrote extensively on prayer and fasting. I remember several occasions on which Edith Schaeffer read from one of Carmichael's books about the subject of prayer or the practice of fasting, giving various helpful suggestions about the observance of such special days or periods. In addition, the Schaeffers were indebted to the ministry and writings of George Mueller and Hudson Taylor on the subjects of prayer and fasting.

Several questions are raised by this brief account of the practice of the Schaeffers, Carmichael, Mueller, and Taylor. Why did these well-known missionaries observe such times of prayer and fasting? How are we to think about extended periods of prayer, such as prayer vigils, when we go away for a night of solitary prayer, or even for several days? Ought all believers to build into our lives such times of going away by ourselves to be alone with the Lord? Should we commit ourselves to special occasions of fasting and prayer?

To begin to answer these questions, we will again observe the practice of Jesus and listen to his teaching on this subject. We will briefly look at the gospel accounts of Jesus' going off to be alone to pray, to see what we can learn from his example. For while it is evident that we are not simply to copy everything Jesus did—we are not all called to be celibate as he was, or to be itinerant preachers, or to die on a cross in our early thirties—it is also clear that we can learn from his example some principles that might be helpful for our own lives. In addition, the apostles command us to imitate the Lord, just as they did (for an example, see 1 Corinthians 11:1 or, even more obviously, Philippians 2:1–11).

WHAT WAS JESUS' PRACTICE?

If we take just a quick glance at the life of Jesus, Scripture clearly reveals that he himself sometimes prayed for lengthy periods. The most obvious of these periods of prayer and fasting when he is away by himself is the forty days of his temptation in the wilderness (Matt. 4:1–11; Mark 1:12–13; Luke 4:1–13).

The other descriptions of such times of solitary prayer are brief mentions in the Synoptic Gospels (Matt. 14:23; Mark 1:35; Luke 5:16; 6:12). In addition, there are the accounts of Jesus' prayers in the garden of Gethsemane (Matt. 26:36–46; Mark 14:32–42; Luke 22:39–46).

One passage specifically states, "In these days he went out to the mountain to pray, and all night he continued in prayer to God" (Luke 6:12); and another says that "he would withdraw to desolate places and pray" (Luke 5:16)—implying that these times of solitary prayer were a regular part of Jesus' life.

LESSONS TO LEARN FROM THESE EXAMPLES

What can we learn from these examples in Jesus' life? In thinking about them and in looking for principles for our own practice, it will be helpful to ask when these periods of extended prayer and fasting took place.

On one of these occasions, Jesus' night of prayer comes immediately before his choosing the twelve apostles from among his disciples (Luke 6:12). Another of these nights of solitary prayer comes right after the feeding of the five thousand (Matt. 14:23). Yet another of these times comes after a period of very intensive healing and casting out of demons, which took place very early in Christ's ministry (Mark 1:32–35). Mark gives this account of the previous evening:

> They brought to him all who were sick or oppressed by demons. And the whole city was gathered together at the door. And he healed many who were sick with various diseases, and cast out many demons. . . . And

95

> rising very early in the morning, while it was still dark,
> he departed and went out to a desolate place, and there
> he prayed. (Mark 1:32–35)

The account that refers to Jesus' habit of withdrawing for extended times of prayer accompanies a description of the great success of his ministry:

> But now even more the report about him went abroad,
> and great crowds gathered to hear him and to be healed
> of their infirmities. But he would withdraw to desolate
> places and pray. (Luke 5:15–16)

The solitary prayers in Gethsemane come, of course, right before Jesus' arrest, his trial, and his death. The most extended time, the forty days of the temptation in the wilderness, comes immediately after his baptism in the Jordan River and just before his public ministry is to begin.

A clear pattern emerges from even a brief examination of these texts. During periods of preparation for his ministry; at major turning points in his life; at moments of significant decision-making; at times of great pressure from success and the expectations of others; on occasions when his teaching and healing were especially dramatic—at these periods in his life, Jesus would withdraw by himself to pray. These appear to be the times when the Son of God knew that he was in particular need of his Father's help, support, strength, and wisdom.

JESUS' NEED AND PRACTICE—HOW MUCH MORE OUR NEED!

If this was so for Jesus, who was perfect in every way, then how much more should this be true for us! Of course we are in desperate need all the time! Not a day passes that we do not need the Lord's wisdom, strength, support, and help. In our need we are encouraged by the Lord through his apostle James that we can always ask for help in our ignorance and uncertainty about what to do:

> If any of you lacks wisdom, let him ask God, who gives generously to all without reproach, and it will be given him. (James 1:5)

We also know that we always need the help of the Holy Spirit, and Jesus promises that the Father will give him to us whenever we ask (Luke 11:13).

Yet in addition to this "always" being in need of wisdom and help, some points in our lives are of particular significance and special need: times of making major decisions for our lives. These occasions are turning points. We can all note such points: marriage, the birth of a child, leaving home for college or seminary or work, taking a new job, searching for a ministry position—any time of major life transition.

To this list we can add other significant situations: periods of life when we face unusually powerful temptations; moments in ministry, business, or school when we must properly deal with success or else risk becoming proud and self-sufficient; and times of special blessing, such as the ongoing growth of a church or other ministry. There are also, of course, stretches of time in which we find ourselves acutely and uncomfortably aware of how miserably evil we are; and there are inevitably times of grief and trouble that threaten to overwhelm us.

Scripture encourages us to seek God when we are in such times of particular need, when we are undertaking a new stage of our service in God's kingdom, when we see our lives to be full of God's blessing, or when we are experiencing severe trials. At such times, we—as individuals, as families, as churches, as a seminary community, as businesses, as schools, or as the people of God in a nation—sense crisis coming, or we feel a deep need to turn to the Lord for his help, or we know that we should give ourselves to celebration and thanksgiving. It is clear that at such seasons of life, extended times of prayer may well be appropriate.

On all such occasions in our lives, we need to be intentional about setting aside an hour or several hours or a day or a night to be alone for extended periods of prayer. These are also times when it is appropriate to include a period of fasting. In addition to the gospel accounts of his life, Jesus also explicitly teaches on this subject. He tells us that he expects us to imitate him in fasting, for he says, "When you fast" (Matt. 6:16), rather than "If you fast." And he expects us to imitate him in extended times of private prayer, for he says: "When you pray, go into your room and shut the door and pray to your Father who is in secret" (Matt. 6:6).

This brief survey of Jesus' practice, and its application to our lives, teaches us that we should indeed be prepared to set aside special days or seasons for fasting and for extended prayer. The fundamental meaning of such fasting is the recognition that our greatest need of all (even greater than our need for regular meals) is the wisdom, strength, support, comfort, and encouragement of our heavenly Father.

NOT BY BREAD ALONE

In the context of his own fasting, Jesus rebukes the devil by telling him that we do not live by bread alone but by every word that has come from God (Matt. 4:4). This rebuke for Satan is also a salutary reminder for us. Our lives are to be governed by our love for the Lord and our desire to honor him through obedience to his command-ments, not by anything else—not by money, career (even a career in ministry), success, pleasure, or the pursuit of our personal happiness; not even by the absolute necessity of food to keep us alive in this world. Fasting helps us to focus on this. In all ministries and churches, in all of our lives, in our businesses and in our homes, we need to have times of fasting and prayer so that we recall what life is about: serving God alone.

I want to suggest that it is needful for every professing Christian, whatever his or her ministry—whether in the church, on a college campus, or in business—to set aside days of fasting and prayer as a reminder that our work is not about the bottom line of its finances, its number in attendance, or its success—it is about pleasing the Lord, about committing myself and all my decisions to obedience to his laws, to the practice of justice, mercy, and faithful-ness, to the seeking of the kingdom of God. We can make money in business or law or medicine or ministry. We can be successful. We can preach great sermons in Jesus' name. We can do many mighty works. But if we are not seeking his kingdom and his righteousness, he is not pleased, and he will say to us: "Depart from me, you workers of lawless-ness" (Matt. 7:23).

In every one of our churches, ministries, and businesses, at the seminary where I teach, whatever our place of serving the Lord, we need such days of fasting and prayer to call us back to God's plans and vision for our lives and work. In our marriages and families, we need such days of prayer and fasting to draw us into the Lord's presence and to reorient our lives to his priorities and wisdom.

As people called to put our hope in Jesus, if we live alone, or with friends and housemates who together seek to honor God, we need to consider setting aside time for prayer and fasting. Such times challenge us to live not in a way that conforms to the self-centered culture around us, but instead as servants of the living God and as servants of others in imitation of Jesus Christ. It might be helpful for every Christian with a business to set aside days of fasting and prayer as a reminder that one's business is not about the bottom line of its finances—it is about pleasing the Lord, about committing oneself and all business decisions to obedience to his laws and to the practice of justice, mercy, and faithfulness.

ARE WE MAKING GOD PAY ATTENTION?

We must understand, however, that it is not the fasting or length of time we pray that "makes" God listen to us. He is always glad to hear our prayers, whether they are short or long, whether we set aside a protracted time or just take a few minutes, whether we fast or not. The fasts or the vigils are expressions of our sense of crisis, of our great need for the Lord's help, of our realization that he desires our devotion to him, of our commitment to serve and honor him. Fasts or vigils are expressions that these things are more important than anything else in our lives.

Indeed, such periods of fasting and extended prayer are important both for us and for the Lord. For the Lord—for he wants to know that we are aware of our great need for him. He wants to know that we understand that living by his Word is even more necessary for our lives than are our regular meals. For us—such times of prayer and fasting remind us of the purpose of our lives and our faith: we are here to seek the kingdom. But despite their importance to the Lord and to us, our fasting, our extended prayer times, our vigils are not "righteous acts" that make God indebted to answer us. They are to be a response to his love and to our sense of need for him.

BEING ALONE

In addition to the practice of Jesus, we have his specific command. Indeed, it is clear that Jesus expects us to imitate him in this commitment to prayer. He tells us to go off alone and pray and to go off alone and fast, just each of us, by himself or herself, with the Father (Matt. 6:5-6, 16-18). By his example and by his instruction, Jesus explicitly teaches us that, as a regular habit, we are to go somewhere that we can be alone with the Lord when we pray. He does not teach us how often we are to do this, nor does he tell us how long such times must last. It is therefore important that we not develop a set of rules that we then impose on the lives of fellow believers, or on ourselves, and say: "This is how long I must pray, and this is how often."

No passage in the New Testament gives us such a list of requirements—thirty minutes alone with the Lord, five days a week, or whatever it may be. But even though we are given no schedule, rule, or time required, Jesus charges us to go into our room and to shut the door and to pray to our Father who is in secret. Our Father who sees in secret is delighted by this private devotion (Matt. 6:6).

DAILY PRAYER

We may add that Jesus does make one statement about the regularity of our prayers. In the Lord's Prayer, Jesus teaches us that we are to pray: "Give us this day our daily bread" (Matt. 6:11). We need food every day, of course, and so the Lord is encouraging us to pray every day for the needs of that day, to recognize each day of our lives that we are dependent on him for food, for life, for breath, for everything. Even more than we need food each day, we need his love each day; even more than requiring daily nourishment for our bodies, we are dependent on his daily support and help. We need to be aware every day that we do not live by bread alone, but by the Word that he speaks and by the strength that he gives. The Lord himself, then, teaches us to pray every day, just as we need to eat every day, for he alone is the source of our life.

UNCEASING PRAYER

The apostle Paul adds another note about the frequency of prayer. He tells us that we are to pray "without ceasing" (ESV) or to pray "continually" (NIV) (1 Thess. 5:17). Here again Paul's point, just like the Lord's, is that we need our faithful Savior's work in our lives all the time. Without his power sustaining us every moment, we would cease to exist, for in him all things (including us) hold together. Without his grace forgiving us, we would be overwhelmed by his righteous anger at our constantly cold hearts and our faltering zeal. Without his Spirit enabling us, and being our constant guide, companion, and friend, we would turn far more often to our own self-centered ways. Growing in grace means a steadily increasing awareness of this moment-by-moment dependence. But the truth is that we are forgetful and self-focused, and so such prayer without ceasing does not come naturally to us. One day, when we are made new and whole, prayer will come as naturally to us as breathing and eating. Until then we have to remind ourselves to pray, and we need to ask the Lord to help us remember to pray, to pray as if we were walking with him in the garden of Eden, or as we will pray when the veil between us is gone.

WILL OUR FASTING OR OUR SPIRITUAL DISCIPLINE IN PRAYER REMOVE THE VEIL?

Of course, such continual prayer does not come naturally to any of us, for a veil has hidden the Lord from us ever since the fall. Unlike Adam and Eve, we no longer experience God walking with us in the cool of the day. Should we expect or hope that the extra time we spend in prayer on a special prayer day, or our commitment to fasting, or our desire to pray without ceasing, will somehow break this barrier down? Should we expect or hope that we can guarantee rich experiences of the presence of God, and that we will discover ourselves walking with him in the garden? Will removal of the veil be realized by our prayers?

We must ask whether it is actually biblical, or at all legitimate, to think of prayer as seeking for ways to remove the veil and so find means of trying to directly experience God. Does God ever call us to do this in his Word? Can we actually accomplish such a thing by finding the right spiritual disciplines or the best method of contemplative prayer or of fasting or private devotion? Surely the disclosure of God's presence is something that is up to him and is not something that we can bring about, no matter how hard we try, no matter how long our prayer vigils, no matter how severe our fasting.

If we consider the experiences of the veil between God and us being removed, they are all sovereign acts of God—such as Paul's being caught up into the third heaven

(2 Cor. 12:1–4) and the extraordinary visions given to John, recorded in the book of Revelation, when the Spirit enables him to see through a door into heaven. Paul even tells us that he is not permitted to describe what he saw. We may speculate, perhaps appropriately, that the reason is that too many of us would try any means we could invent to remove the veil so that we also might see what Paul saw. All such experiences, however, wonderful as they most certainly are, are in the control of God and not of us. We cannot cause such visions to happen, and we cannot twist God's arm to manipulate him into giving us dramatic and unusual experiences.

THE CHALLENGE OF OUR REBELLIOUS PERSONAL INDEPENDENCE AND AUTONOMY

In addition to this present reality of God's being hidden from us, we also do not have the desire to be in his presence or to talk with him all the time—indeed, we do not have such a desire most of the time. Because the heart of sin is pride and self-centeredness, we are not by nature, in our present state, eager to know God. Perhaps we long to be eager to know him. Perhaps there are occasional moments when we long to be praying constantly and naturally, just as breathing and eating come naturally to us. But this is not who we are.

This good that we long for—of desiring to know God well and of being faithful in prayer—is always accompanied by the ongoing sad reality of our coldness of heart, of our reluctance, of our self-focused lives, and of our lack of faith. Whenever we try to pray aright, we find this other principle at work within us, so that the good of praying continually that we long to do we do not do, and the evil of praying so occasionally and so little is what we regularly do. See Paul's words about himself as a mature believer, as an apostle (Rom. 7:15–23). I have simply applied these words of Paul to our prayer life. I do not think that I have ever met a Christian who would deny the truth of my words about our reluctance to know God well, or of our lack of zeal in prayer.

THE ADDITIONAL CHALLENGE OF OUR CULTURE

We also face another difficulty: living in this particular culture at this moment in history. Our society has taught us far too well that we are to live for ourselves. It has drummed into our minds and hearts that we are not to live to serve God, that we are not living before the face of God, that we are not accountable to him. All societies have been full of sin and of the reluctance to worship God, but this radically secular approach to human life is unique to our time.

Our culture has brainwashed us into believing that we exist in this world to pursue our own personal happiness; it has fooled us into thinking that true freedom and fulfillment arise only from living for our individual wants and desires. Most believers, as well as everyone else around us, are convinced that we are in control of our own lives—though as Christians we must know that such a conviction is absurd! The consequence is that we all live much of the time as if we were self-existent and self-supporting—as if we could get by just fine without the Lord.

This mentality of "I will do it myself; I don't need the Lord"—what we might call the mind-set of a two-year-old—

is the very heart and essence of the fall, of the original sin, of Satan's temptation of Adam and Eve. The emphasis of our culture sanctifies the belief in self-love, the longing for self-satisfaction, and the pursuit of my individual happiness as if this were the greatest truth ever discovered by the human race. With this emphasis shaping all our thoughts, we become crippled in prayer.

This, sadly, is who we are. We are those who no longer realize that we are designed to live as people who are always holding on to our Father's hand (as a two-year-old needs to do, but is often reluctant to do); created to be those who are always eager to do what pleases him; shaped from the beginning to be always knowing that we need his wisdom, his input, his love, his guiding hand, his strengthening of our purpose, of our will, of our heart, of our whole being. Dependence does not come naturally to us as fallen people, and even less naturally as twenty-first-century postmodern Americans. This is the most basic reason why we find prayer so problematic. This is one of the simplest, and saddest, explanations of why we pray so little.

THE EXAMPLE OF JESUS—HIS DEPENDENCE ON THE FATHER

In Jesus we see exactly the opposite of this mentality. He declares that his food is to do the will of the One who sent him (John 4:34), that he speaks only the words the Father wants him to speak, and that he does only what the Father wants him to do (John 12:49–50; 14:24, 31). Isaiah contains a beautiful statement about the coming Messiah, the Christ. He is pictured as One whose first waking thought each morning is to listen to his heavenly Father's voice, and to be taught by him:

The Sovereign LORD has given me an instructed
    tongue,
  to know the word that sustains the weary.
He wakens me morning by morning,
  wakens my ear to listen like one being taught.
The Sovereign LORD has opened my ears, and I have
    not been rebellious; I have not drawn back.
  (Isa. 50:4–5 NIV)

Here is Jesus, the eternal Son of God, the second person of the Trinity, the Creator of all worlds, praying without ceasing; delighting in his dependence on his Father; eager to hear his Lord's words of instruction; always willing to set his own will and plans on one side, and ready to do instead what the Father has for him on each particular day and in every setting in which he finds himself.

FASTING AND PRAYER ARE NOT WORKS, BUT AN EXPRESSION OF LOVE AND DEPENDENCE

Our aim, our prayer, must be that we might begin to see that we were made to be like Jesus; that we might begin to enjoy our need of the Father's love and help; that we might gladly choose not to fight him, not to resist him, and not to resist our need of him.

This is why we must be disciplined in prayer: to be full of joy in the knowledge that we depend on our Father—not so that we can measure how spiritual we are, or feel proud of ourselves because we have ticked off a list of the number of minutes, hours, and occasions we have prayed.

No, discipline in prayer has to do with reminding ourselves, moment by moment, how much we truly need the Lord. It is a matter of developing a consistent mealtime

107

pattern of saying "thank you" to the Lord; a habit when we rise in the morning of telling him we love him and need him; a routine when we walk by the way (or drive along the way) that we long for him to guide and direct us; a custom when we meet people of asking him to help us to know what to say and to do; an instant recognition that when we face temptation we must turn to him for strength; a glad remembrance at the end of each day, when we lie down at night, that we are thankful for his support and that we are sorry for our failures. This is the discipline we need.

Entering such reminders in our calendars, our day-timers, our diaries, our to-do lists may indeed be helpful to us, though it should not be necessary. I don't need a list of reminders to eat three times a day! Indeed, I need reminding to eat less often and to consume less when I do eat. But this again is our problem: we need the Lord more than we need those three meals, and yet we forget. So anything we can do that will keep that reminder in the forefront of our thoughts should help us be more disciplined.

Yet a word of caution is needed. Personal discipline in any area of our life has value. But legalism (making a set of rules that measure how well we are doing in praying regularly) will not help because it almost always leads to either pride or despondency: pride because we are keeping the rules, and so we congratulate ourselves and become puffed up about how spiritual we are compared with others or with our own previous practice; or despondency because we are not keeping our rules, and so we feel unspiritual, useless, and condemned. The Lord desires neither pride nor despondency from us.

We are always to remember that the Lord will not hear us better because we have observed our disciplines.

This is a truth that we need to have engraved on our hearts and minds. Nor will the Lord hear us less well because we have not kept to the letter of our disciplines for prayer. He is our completely loving Father who does not condemn us and who will not turn us away because of our lack of spiritual discipline. It is just because he loves us that he desires that we set time aside for prayer, and that we fast from time to time. He longs for us to show him how much we love him and how much we are aware that we need him.

Questions for Reflection and Discussion

1. Have you found discipline in prayer easy, or do you struggle with regular prayer, daily prayer, or prayer without ceasing?

2. Are there books on prayer or on fasting that have been particularly helpful to you? (As for me, the most helpful teaching I have heard or read has come from C. S. Lewis, from Francis and Edith Schaeffer and Amy Carmichael, and from Bryan Chappell and David Calhoun, two of my colleagues at Covenant Theological Seminary.)

3. As you think about the issue of imitating Jesus, what are the aspects of his life that you think every Christian should imitate, and what are the aspects of his life that are not appropriate to seek to imitate?

4. Have you been attracted to the idea that if we pray in just the right way, we might be able to "remove the

veil"? Do you think this idea is right or wrong? Use Scripture to defend your view.

5. In what areas do you think you have been impacted by our culture's emphasis on personal autonomy, on living with control over one's own life, and on the right to define happiness and personal fulfillment for oneself?

6. As you think about the year ahead of you, when might it be appropriate to set aside a time of extended prayer and fasting?

7

THE TEMPTATION OF JESUS—INTRODUCTION

Matthew 3:13–4:11

In the last chapter, we began our reflections by looking at those times when Jesus went off alone to pray or to fast and pray. It is obvious as we think about his life that the longest extended period of fasting and prayer was the forty days of his temptation in the wilderness. In this chapter, we look in more detail at that particular episode in Jesus' life.

We read in the gospels that Jesus was committed to "fulfill[ing] all righteousness" (Matt. 3:15), for he was the One who came to be our representative as the last Adam, the perfect man, One like us, yet without sin. This eagerness to fulfill all righteousness led Jesus to the Jordan to be baptized by John. He wanted to show his full identification with those he had come to serve and to save, so he joined the line to receive the baptism of repentance, even though he had done nothing for which he needed to repent. Rather, he was declaring himself to be one with us, his people. This identification with sinners points forward to the baptism of Jesus' death—the central purpose of his coming into the world.

Ritual washings or "baptisms" were also required of the priests as they took up their terms of service in the temple. There in the sanctuary they worked at duties in which they would be the representatives of the people before God. They were washed because they were sinners who needed to be cleansed before they entered the Lord's presence to serve him as the advocates of their people. Jesus was also baptized as a priest taking up his duties, at the onset of his priestly and prophetic ministry, once again identifying himself with those who need cleansing and as his people's representative.

His baptism was accompanied by the descent of the Spirit in the form of a dove. This sign of the Spirit's coming on him was a clear testimony to Jesus' intention to live his life, and to carry out his ministry, in humble dependence on the power of the Spirit in all he was about to undertake. To all those assembled by the Jordan that day, the Father demonstrated his delight in his Son, by sending the Spirit in visible form to light on him, and by audibly declaring his love and favor from heaven:

> This is my beloved Son, with whom I am well pleased.
> (Matt. 3:17)

WHAT DOES IT MEAN THAT JESUS IS CALLED THE "SON OF GOD"?

One interpretative question arises that will be important for our reflections on Jesus' temptation: what did it mean for Jesus to be called by the Father "my beloved Son, with whom I am well pleased"? Is this a designation of Jesus as the eternal Son of God, the second person of the Trinity? Or is this a designation that he is the messianic Son, the King of God's people? I want to suggest that both elements are present. The heavenly voice quotes Isaiah:

> Behold my servant, whom I uphold, my chosen, in whom my soul delights. (Isa. 42:1)

This is a passage about the messianic Servant whom God will send to bring salvation to his people, Israel, and light to the Gentiles. But there are also echoes of the second psalm:

> "As for me, I have set my King
>   on Zion, my holy hill."
>
> I will tell of the decree:
> The LORD said to me, "You are my Son; today I have
>   begotten you." (Ps. 2:6–7)

This is a psalm about the messianic King whom the Lord will set on Zion to rule Israel and all the nations. God declares this King to be his Son in fulfillment of the promise made in God's covenant with David (2 Sam. 7:12–16).

There are also echoes of Abraham's offering his son Isaac and, in particular, of the words of the Angel of the Lord to Abraham as he repeats the promises of the covenant:

> By myself I have sworn, declares the LORD, because you have done this and have not withheld your son, your only son, I will surely bless you, and I will surely multiply your offspring as the stars of heaven and as the sand that is on the seashore. (Gen. 22:15–17)

The echo of the words of the Angel of the Lord to Abraham opens up the possibility that at the baptism the Father is declaring that Jesus is his Son, the One who has been beloved by him through all eternity. This recalling of the words of God to Abraham also points forward to the cross when the Father will offer up his only beloved Son as a sacrifice for sin.

It is right, then, to assume that the words of the Father at Jesus' baptism can be understood to refer both to the eternal sonship of the second person of the Trinity and to Jesus as the descendant of David who is designated as the messianic King and Son of God.

It is immediately after this public declaration by the Father—that Jesus is indeed the Son of God—that the temptation occurs. Jesus has been assured of the Father's love, favor, and blessing, and then he faces severe testing.

BLESSING FOLLOWED BY TESTING

How often this is the situation in which our most troubling temptations come! When God has blessed us in wonderful ways, Satan comes to test us, for he knows how easily our hearts become proud and how hardened to God's purposes, precisely because we have experienced such blessing. We forget the Giver of good gifts and the One who has honored us. Instead, we reflect on our own worth and our own giftedness without reference to the Father, when, in truth, he is the One who is the source of all that is good in our lives.

In Jesus' case, of course, his heart was not proud and hard like ours, but it is clear that Satan's longing is always to turn those he tempts toward self-love and self-worship, and away from the worship of the Creator. We may assume that the devil came to try to deflect Jesus from the path of serving his Father, just as he is constantly at work seeking to turn us away from God's purposes. In our lives he knows that our successes and triumphs are our times of greatest weakness. He knows this because he himself turned from worshiping God to self-worship when he became proud of his own glory. This was how he tempted Adam and Eve. In like manner, he hopes to turn Jesus aside from his chosen path of humble service of his Father. He plans to tempt our Lord just as he himself was tempted.

We should note that we do not read that after his baptism, and after the demonstrations of his Father's approval, Jesus said: "Now I am ready to do battle with Satan." No such arrogance characterized him; he had no such desire to put God to the test! Rather, the Spirit, who has come to empower him for his ministry, leads him out to the wilderness where he is to undergo the temptations.

We need to learn this from Jesus: we are not to throw ourselves in the path of temptation just because we have felt the Father's pleasure. Temptations will come because there is an enemy, an adversary, an accuser, a tempter who delights to destroy our souls and to turn God's children away from him. We do not need to rush headlong into temptation; we do not need to challenge the devil to a duel; nor do we need to go out into the wilderness of this world seeking trouble! Plenty of troubles and temptations will come our way in due time.

For Jesus, this time in the wilderness was not the only time that the devil tempted him. Luke's account tells us that the devil "departed from him until an opportune time" (Luke 4:13), but this episode we know as "the temptation" constitutes Satan's most serious and prolonged assault on Jesus' trust and obedience. We should also note that this account is the only record we have of Jesus and the devil in direct personal conversation and face-to-face encounter.

ARE FACE-TO-FACE ENCOUNTERS NORMATIVE?

This raises the question whether we ourselves should expect the same kind of face-to-face confrontations with the devil. How should we respond to such a question? I think we have to recognize that there are various aspects of Jesus' prayer life that we should not assume will be precisely mirrored in ours.

For example, Jesus hears a voice from heaven speaking directly to him, a voice that is also publicly audible. This happens on two occasions that are recorded for us: first, at Jesus' baptism; second, when Jesus was in Jerusalem at the Feast of Passover. On this second occasion, the words from heaven come in response to Jesus' prayer:

> "Father, glorify your name." Then a voice came from heaven: "I have glorified it, and I will glorify it again." (John 12:28)

Jesus then comments that the voice came not for his sake, but for those present. In addition to these publicly audible words from heaven, we also read of Jesus' two-way conversation with Satan during the temptation in the wilderness. On these occasions the veil that is usually drawn between the seen and unseen worlds is set aside. But these unveilings of what is normally hidden are unusual even in the life of Christ.

Of course, other similar examples of the pulling aside of the veil are recorded for us. We read of these extraordinary happenings taking place in the lives of a handful

of New Testament believers: the appearance of the angel
Gabriel to Mary; the appearance of the angel to Zechariah;
the dreams of Joseph, both before and after the birth of
Christ, in which an angel speaks to him; the heavenly host
proclaiming the birth of the Messiah to the shepherds; the
vision of Paul when he is taken up into the third heaven;
Christ's appearance to Paul on the Damascus road; the
visions of the apostle John that enabled him to write the
book of Revelation.

These few examples and all such similar encounters
recorded in the Old and New Testaments are clearly not
to be considered normative or regulative, in the sense that
all believers are to expect them to be a part of normal or
everyday Christian life. Most of these occur at particularly
important junctures in the history of salvation—this is true of
the appearance of angels in the early chapters of the gospels
and of the appearance of Christ to Saul. It is true of the
extraordinary events associated with the calling of Moses
and of the miraculous happenings during the ministries of
Elijah and Elisha.

In addition, we are taught at no point that we are to ask
for such visions or voices from heaven. Nor are we promised
anywhere that we can look for such things to happen—for
the veil to be drawn back that hides the unseen world from
us. If anything, biblical teaching comes down on the other
side of this question. For example, we are commanded by
Paul not to let those who take their stand on visions dis-
qualify us from being confident of Christ's love for us, or of
our status as his beloved (see Col. 2:18-19). Indeed, in this
passage Paul makes it clear that he thinks the visions and
angels that such people speak about are not genuine at all,
but rather the irrational ballooning of their own senses and
minds. Paul's comments require us never to judge our own

spiritual status, or anyone else's, by the claim of experiencing the unveiling of the unseen and unheard world—whether those claims are genuine or false.

The Gospels contain a fascinating passage that instructs us here. Jesus has sent the seventy-two out to teach and to minister ahead of him in the towns that he is about to visit (Luke 10:1–2). They return full of joy, declaring to Jesus that "even the demons are subject to us in your name!" (v. 17). He assures them that he did see Satan falling like lightning from heaven and that he has given them authority over all the power of the enemy (vv. 18–19). Then Jesus adds some striking words:

> Nevertheless, do not rejoice in this, that the spirits are subject to you, but rejoice that your names are written in heaven. (Luke 10:20)

Jesus' charge is very clear: even when we experience the unveiling of the unseen world, even when we see extraordinary things take place, we are not to put our hope in these events, no matter how glorious they may be. Rather, we are to put our hope in the most basic truths of the gospel: the forgiveness of our sins and the assurance of the life to come. These are ours through faith in Jesus. What we are to rejoice in is the common and normative heritage of all Christian believers, not the particular or even the most special experiences that God may grant us.

We may go further and add that if the Lord does give us wonderful visions, then he may well supplement them with severe thorns in the flesh to prevent us from becoming too elated by the "surpassing greatness of the revelations" (2 Cor. 12:7–9). Reading of the seriousness of Paul's struggles, I am not sure that I am eager to ask for visions and revelations of surpassing greatness! But whether we desire such experiences or not, regardless of the possible cost, the fundamental point is sure: we are not promised visions and voices, either of the Lord or of the devil. The occasional experience of Jesus is not normative for us. The devil will certainly tempt us—of this we may be sure. But we should not expect, nor should we desire, to see him with our own eyes or to hear him with our own ears.

THE SETTING OF THE TEMPTATIONS

The temptations take place in the wilderness, the place where John is described as doing his work of ministry, a place that is far away from the cities and centers of power, far away from the comforts of home and civilization. Jesus is alone there, apart from his family and friends. He has no human companions to whom he can turn for strength, encouragement, or comfort. No food is available for him to eat. He is there in the wilderness to fast, to pray, to prepare himself for his public ministry, and to face temptation—temptation in particular about how his ministry is to be accomplished.

What of us? Are we to imitate Jesus' example of going off by himself and fasting for such an extended period? As we saw in our previous chapter, it is quite clear that we are to be ready to fast as part of a regular pattern in our life of prayer. Two particular accounts of fasting and prayer in the life of the churches are recorded for us in the book of Acts (Acts 13:1–3; 14:21–23). The first comes at a time when the church in Antioch is seeking God's wisdom and grace as it sends out Paul and Barnabas for the first great missionary journey. This is a turning point in the history of the advance of the gospel of Christ. The second example is particularly interesting, for it describes something that is a regular part of the life of any new or growing church. Paul and Barnabas make a return visit to each of the churches that had come into being as a consequence of their missionary work. They encourage and strengthen the disciples, challenging them to remain faithful to Christ despite the tribulation that they should expect to come. Then Luke adds these words:

> And when they had appointed elders for them in every church, with prayer and fasting they committed them to the Lord in whom they had believed. (Acts 14:23)

The implication of this brief description is that the pattern of fasting and prayer should be seen as normal for our churches in any situation such as the ordination of new elders.

Adding this to our study in the last chapter, it should be evident that fasting ought to be an ordinary part of the individual believer's life, and a regular part of the life of each congregation. But the question remains: "Does the pattern of fasting that we should adopt for our lives mean that we all ought to plan a forty-day fast in imitation of Jesus?" Several points need to be made in response to this question.

JESUS' UNIQUE CALLING

We should observe first that the text is drawing parallels between the experience of Jesus and some episodes in the life of the Israelites. The people of Israel were called to wander in the wilderness for forty years—forty years in which we see repeated examples of their unbelief, of their rebellion against God, and of their disobedience to his commandments. Moses spent forty years in the wilderness being prepared for the ministry to which God was calling him, and he spent forty days and nights fasting and praying on Sinai. We also read that Elijah fasted for "forty days and forty nights" when he was fleeing from Jezebel (1 Kings 19:8) and that he spent a lengthy time in the wilderness reflecting on his mission and ministry. It should be clear to us that Jesus is the new Israel. He is the representative of God's people who serves the Lord faithfully during his time in the wilderness—the place where the nation was unfaithful. Jesus is the new Moses, for he is himself the Lawgiver and Judge. In addition, Jesus is the new Elijah who, like Elijah, faces opposition, but who, unlike Elijah, endures his trials without the loss of faith and hope.

There are, then, some unique elements present in the ministry of Jesus and in his very lengthy fast in the wilderness. Such lengthy fasting is not a pattern for our lives required of us by the Scriptures, any more than Jesus' celibacy, his itinerant teaching ministry, his many healings, or his death on the cross are to be considered a spiritual pattern or a requirement for all Christians. Nor are these unique parts of Jesus' life a requirement for those who consider themselves to be particularly committed holy "athletes." Jesus' life has many unrepeatable practices and episodes.

While Christ's ministry is unique, and we are not called to copy this aspect of it precisely, it may well be that extended periods of fasting will be a particular calling for some members of God's people at particular moments in the history of redemption and in the history of the spread of the church across the world.

Yet no Christian should even consider undertaking a forty-day fast for the reason of trying to prove something about his or her spiritual powers of endurance. If I get lost at sea, or isolated away from food, and have of necessity to endure such a lengthy fast, then God is quite capable of caring for me. In the history of the church we can find examples of believers who have been cared for and have survived such extreme hunger.

It is also necessary to add that no Christian should try to practice a severe fast of even several days without first getting medical advice. Tragedies have occurred when Christians have unwisely fasted for too long. Spiritual eagerness should never set aside the need for practical advice and wisdom.

If I think I am being called to lengthy fasting, I must be quite sure that I am being obedient to the calling of the Lord, rather than practicing some self-made religion. Many times in the history of the church, people have imposed on themselves, and on others, very strict demands about food, about sex, or about severe treatment of the body, and have done this by insisting that such practices are a superior form of spiritual discipline. The apostle Paul speaks against this with great passion in his letter to the Colossians. He is writing in the context of various regulations that the "super-spiritual" teachers have imposed: "Do not handle, Do not taste, Do not touch" (Col. 2:21). These regulations, he says, are simply

> according to human precepts and teachings[.] These have indeed an appearance of wisdom in promoting self-made religion and asceticism and severity to the body, but they are of no value in stopping the indulgence of the flesh [here "flesh" refers to the sinful nature]. (Col. 2:22b–23)

The Scripture completely rejects asceticism, that is, the harsh treatment of the body, as if this were a means to spiritual growth. So fasting must not be undertaken as if it were the way either to measure one's spirituality or to become more spiritual. When we fast, we must fast for scriptural reasons—not for our self-made religion, or in obedience to any human traditions that have specific rules about spiritual maturity. We may, then, take extended times of prayer and fasting—but there is no need for us, and no call for us, to take a forty-day fast as if this were to be our typical calling.

LENGTHY PERIODS ALONE?

We must assume that once Jesus is led into the wilderness by the Spirit, his forty days is spent in prayer and in reflection on his coming ministry and on his Father's purposes for him. None of us could possibly endure such a lengthy period alone without the special grace of the Lord. We can, of course, read many stories of those Christians who have been forced into solitary confinement as punishment, and who then testify to God's care during such a time. This does not mean, however, that we should seek such lengthy periods of solitude or that we should put God to the test by trying to imitate Jesus in this. The calling of the hermit, the solitary saint who spends his life alone in prayer and meditation, is not one that we can legitimately draw from this text.

Most of us will find ourselves facing particular personal problems if we have to spend too much time alone—for indeed, it is not good for us to be alone for any great length of time. It is when Adam is alone, and he realizes his aloneness, that we find the first "not good" in the biblical story. Even though Adam has an unbroken fellowship with God, humanly speaking he is alone, and this is declared to be "not good." It is not good for us to be alone because the Lord has created and redeemed us for human relationships, and his will for us is that we grow in love for others. So often when we are alone, when we are not living with others whom we are called to serve, we become self-centered, unhappy with the Father's plans for us, questioning his will and his goodness. We also find ourselves facing extra temptations. This is one of the reasons that Paul writes as he does about a husband and wife belonging to each other sexually:

> Do not deprive one another, except perhaps by agreement for a limited time, that you may devote yourselves to prayer; but then come together again, so that Satan may not tempt you because of your lack of self-control. (1 Cor. 7:5)

Our isolation brings out the worst in us. Christian obedience requires us to commit most of our lives to the service of others—and this is, of course, how Jesus spent the greater part of his life.

Because Jesus shares our humanity, it should be no surprise that in this time of aloneness he endures the most severe temptations. He was indeed tempted in every way as we are, yet he was without sin. Was it easy for him to resist the temptations with which the devil attacked him? Not according to the Scripture. Hebrews teaches us that he agonized over the challenges that confronted him, that he wept and cried out, and that he struggled to learn obedience (Heb. 5:7-8).

Yet unlike the first human pair, Adam and Eve, when they faced temptation in the garden of Eden, this second Adam resists the temptations that come to him. I refer to Jesus as the second Adam because we are intended to see the parallel with Adam and Eve, and also to see the contrast between them and Jesus. Adam and Eve were the ancestors and heads of the human race: they listened to the voice of the tempter, succumbed to his temptation, and turned to a life of disobedience. In Adam and Eve we all died (1 Cor. 15:22), for they were our representatives. Their faithlessness, their disobedience, their defeat by the devil are accounted to us.

Jesus comes to take up the fight once more, a new Adam to be the new Head of our human race: he refuses to listen to the voice of the tempter, he resists temptation, and he lives a life of full and perfect obedience. In Christ we are all made alive (1 Cor. 15:22), for he is our new representative: his faithfulness, his obedience, his victory over the devil are accounted to us.

Jesus also comes to the struggle in the wilderness as the new leader, the descendant of David, the true King, the final and perfect representative of the people of God. We read this account, and as was noted earlier, we hear echoes of Moses' forty days and nights on Mount Sinai when he fasted and prayed for Israel (Ex. 24:18; 34:28; Deut. 9:9, 18) and of Elijah's forty days and nights of fasting as he journeyed to Horeb, the Mount of God, the same location as Sinai (1 Kings 19:8).

Moses and Elijah are two of the greatest leaders of God's people in the Old Testament period—the one standing at the head of the people as political leader and lawgiver, the other as the head of the line of prophets speaking God's Word to the people and calling them to obedience. Jesus is the new leader and Lawgiver; he is the new and greatest of the prophets. It is fitting for him as the new Head and representative of God's people to endure what these earlier leaders had endured. He is also the promised King in the line of David.

Another way to summarize these points would be to say that Jesus is the fulfillment and perfect expression of all that the Scripture teaches us about obedience, about righteousness, and about representation of the true Israel by the leaders of that chosen nation, God's covenant people. As leaders whose life and ministry were an antetype of Christ, it is not surprising that later in Jesus' life Moses and Elijah discuss with him his coming death when they appear with him at his transfiguration (see Matt. 17:1–8).

Questions for Reflection and Discussion

1. Have you wondered about Jesus' being baptized, when John's baptism was a baptism of repentance for the forgiveness of sins, and whether and why such a baptism was appropriate for Jesus?

2. Was the thought that there are two possible meanings for the title "Son of God" a new idea for you? How would you try to respond to a Jehovah's Witness, or to anyone else, who claimed that "Son of God" always refers to Jesus only as the Messiah, the One who would be declared to be God's Son because he was the messianic King?

3. Have you experienced in your own life that times of great blessing have sometimes been followed by severe temptation? Were you aware at the time this happened of any connection between the two?

4. Have you ever purposely thrown yourself into the way of temptation, knowing that you were going to fall into

sin? This question is obviously difficult to discuss with others, but even if you cannot discuss it openly, it is important to confess such things to the Lord.

5. Are you troubled by the idea that amazing spiritual experiences are not normative for all Christians? Why do you think Paul writes that he is not permitted to describe his experience of being caught up into the third heaven?

6. What is your response to the teaching in this chapter that Christ is the new Adam, the new Israel, the new Priest, the new Moses, the new Elijah, the new David? Why is this teaching important?

7. Have you ever been attracted to the teaching that we ought to treat our bodies severely in order to help ourselves resist sin? How would you respond to someone who sought to draw you to such an approach to spiritual growth?

8

The Nature of the Temptations

Matthew 4:1–11

Jesus comes to the time of temptation in the wilderness as the second Adam, the Lawgiver greater than Moses, the foremost of the prophets (even greater than Elijah), the Priest of his people, the true Son of David, the representative of God's holy nation. What are the particular ways that Satan tempts the new champion of our race, the new leader of God's people, during these forty days?

"Command These Stones to Become Bread"

The first temptation seems very straightforward. Jesus is hungry after his prolonged fast, so Satan simply says: "If you are the Son of God, command these stones to become loaves of bread" (Matt. 4:3). The devil knows that Jesus has just been publicly declared to be God's Son by the voice

THE HEART OF PRAYER

from heaven. What could be more natural than to use his power as the eternal Son, and his favored status as the messianic King, to meet his needs? "Your power as God's Son," Satan suggests, "is not only for others, but for your own use, too. Surely nothing could be more reasonable than to satisfy your hunger by your supernatural power." Beneath the surface of this temptation is the devil's suggestion that Jesus should use his "invisible attributes, namely, his eternal power and divine nature" (Rom. 1:20), for himself, to meet whatever needs or wants he has as a man. He encourages Jesus to grasp onto his divine power for himself, to cling to it for his own advantage—precisely what Paul teaches us that Jesus chose not to do:

> Though he was in the form of God, [he] did not count equality with God a thing to be grasped, but made himself nothing, taking the form of a servant, being born in the likeness of men. And being found in human form, he humbled himself by becoming obedient . . . . (Phil. 2:6–8)

Jesus understood that his calling was to live as a man meeting his needs, as all other men and women do, by the labors of his hands, or through the kindness of others. When he performed miracles, it would be by the power of the Spirit in humble dependence on his Father, not by dramatic displays of his own divine nature to meet his own needs. The devil understands that even good gifts, even proper strengths, may be misused for self-centered ends and with improper motivations. So he tests Jesus in this way: "You are God's Son; you are glorious in power. Prove it; show it; why go hungry?"

So many of the temptations we struggle with are like this: we are tempted to take good things that are God's gifts, but by the wrong means, for the wrong ends, or with the wrong motivations. The strengths of one's personality or the greatest gifts one has are the areas where we will be tempted. Most especially, each one of us will be tempted to use our strengths and gifts for ourselves, for our own honor, rather than in the service of God and for the well-being of others.

We will also be tempted to think that if we do not use our gifts and strengths in this way, then the Lord will be depriving us of something that should rightfully be ours. This was the test for Adam and Eve, the proposal that Satan put before them, the suggestion of God's not wishing them to realize their full potential: "Adam and Eve, you can be like God, so go for it!" To this temptation they fell, Eve being deceived and Adam going along with her.

Unlike the first Adam, the second Adam, even though he was fully God, did not think his equality with God was something to be grasped, proved, or displayed for his own advantage. Here in this first temptation, Satan tries to turn Jesus from his path of contentment with his Father's calling and provision. Jesus' response is to quote God's Law:

> It is written, "Man shall not live by bread alone, but by every word that comes from the mouth of God." (Matt. 4:4, quoting Deut. 8:3)

The context of these words is God's provision of manna for the Israelites. Even though God gladly and generously provided bread for the daily needs of the people of Israel, there was one thing far more important—to live in dependence on God and in obedience to him. On another occasion, Jesus tells his disciples:

131

My food is to do the will of him who sent me and to accomplish his work. (John 4:34)

There in the wilderness, Jesus responds to Satan's proposal by stating his dependence on his Father, and his desire to live by walking in his ways. The Father's word, his word that creates and upholds the universe, his word that gives life—this word will meet Jesus' every need and shape his life. Jesus will not use his power for himself, to prove his status, his gifts, or his glory. He will live in the Father's will.

"THROW YOURSELF DOWN"

The second temptation goes further than the first. Satan takes Jesus to the high point of the temple (perhaps 170 feet from the temple roof down to its foundation, but more like 500 feet down to the valley floor below). This time the devil himself quotes Scripture:

> Throw yourself down, for it is written, "He will command his angels concerning you," and "On their hands they will bear you up, lest you strike your foot against a stone." (Matt. 4:6, quoting Ps. 91:11–12)

The devil, of course, knows the Bible, and he is happy to misquote God for his own purposes. Psalm 91 is praising God for his sheltering love and his watchful protection over those who are his. But it is not encouraging us as believers to put God's care for his people to the test by throwing ourselves into harm's way and then expecting him to send his angels for our rescue—though this is how Satan interprets and applies the text. He is the master Scripture-twister!

Sadly, this is also the way that many interpret the promises of God. I will give two examples of people I have met who were taught to understand this text (and others with similar promises) in precisely the way in which Satan expounds it.

The first was a young woman whose pastor had taught her that God's love for us is so great that we can even throw ourselves down from the roof of a tall building and expect his angels to keep us from harm. She took her pastor at his word, and she jumped from the roof of a tall building in Washington, D.C. It was a miracle that she did not die, so in that sense God protected her from the folly of her action and from the Scripture-twisting of her pastor. When she fell, however, she hit a Volkswagen van feet first. She damaged the van severely, but she also smashed the bones in her feet. It was as if the Lord were saying to her: "If you put me to the test, you will indeed strike your foot. My Word is not to be misinterpreted or misapplied in such a way."

My second example is even more tragic. A young man came to visit us at the English L'Abri. He lived just a few miles away in the city of Farnborough in Hampshire in southern England. As I talked to him, he told me that he suffered with a severe form of epilepsy. Under medical supervision, he had been taking heavy doses of medication since early childhood. But he went on to say that he had recently started worshiping at a church that taught that all sicknesses would be healed after the church elders had prayed a "prayer of faith" and laid hands on those who were ill.

His pastor and elders had prayed for him and laid hands on him, and then they had commanded him to throw away all his epilepsy medication. They also told him that in the future, he should feel free to ride a bicycle through the city, and that he could ignore all his doctor's instructions about appropriate behavior for epileptics. (Those with severe epilepsy are told never to watch television or movies, never to drive, never to ride a bicycle in traffic, and so on. The reason for this is that the flashing images of the screen or of moving traffic can trigger an epileptic attack.)

I begged him to keep taking his medication, not to ride his bicycle, and to see his doctor. He took no notice of my pleas, and just a few days later I heard that he had been killed while riding his bicycle during the rush hour in Farnborough. He had become visually disoriented, had had an epileptic attack, and had ridden his bike straight into a bus. The driver was appalled because he had had no time to stop and could not avoid running the bus over the young man.

I tell these shocking stories to remind us how wicked it is to misuse Scripture and to put God to the test—which is precisely what the devil encourages Jesus to do in this second temptation.

In addition, Satan once again appeals to Jesus' knowledge of who he is and to his sense of his special relationship to the Father. He says, in effect: "Go ahead; throw yourself down from the temple pinnacle. The Father would never let you be harmed! He loves you too much." Also, such a dramatic public action would be a spectacular way for Jesus to demonstrate to the crowds at the temple that he was the Messiah: to fall such a vast distance and yet be unharmed. What an extraordinary display of his power and of God the Father's care for him! The people would be struck with awe and wonder; they would say: "This One must be the Messiah; he is the King, the divine Son of whom the psalms speak!"

Again, how often are we tempted in this kind of way? We long to show in dramatic ways that we have faith, that we are God's chosen ones, that we are more special to him than others. I am afraid that many of our secret motivations are warped like this: "Lord, I want to show them! Just let them see how important I am to your purposes and to your kingdom, how precious I am to you."

We may do this with the good gifts of God: desire to teach or otherwise serve well, in order to impress people with a display of our own faith, our own abilities, our own significance to the church of God, and our value to the Lord himself. If we examine our hearts, however, we see that at the wellspring of our actions, our intentions are self-serving and self-exalting. Not only our desire to display our gifts and service, but even the motive behind our prayers may be like this: "Lord, you answer my prayer, and then they will honor you when they see me! (And they will honor me, too.)"

Jesus' response to this second temptation is to expose the hypocrisy in Satan's words:

> You shall not put the Lord your God to the test. (Matt. 4:7, quoting Deut. 6:16)

In this passage that Jesus quotes, Moses refers to the way the people tested God in the wilderness, at Massah, when they grumbled that the Lord was not providing for them and demanded that Moses prove God's care for them by giving them water (Ex. 17:1–7). All such testing of God is deeply displeasing to him, for it displays a lack of true faith, an arrogant presumption on God's kindness, and an ugly self-centeredness.

Jesus knows that there is no shortcut to serving his Father, no easy way to gain the support of the people, no quick and spectacular resolution to his ministry. There is rather faithfulness, doing his Father's will day after day, trusting him in the troubles that come along, believing in his care when times are tough. Any other way is the way of presumption and pride.

"ALL THESE I WILL GIVE YOU, IF YOU WORSHIP ME"

In the third temptation, Satan tries a direct rather than subtle approach. He takes Jesus to the top of a high mountain and shows him (perhaps in a vision) all the kingdoms of the world in a brief moment: "All these I will give you, if you will fall down and worship me" (Matt. 4:9). The devil suggests to Jesus that there is a way to avoid the humiliation, the suffering, and the cross that is planned for him. Instead of attaining his crown through service and death, the devil will give him a crown immediately—if Jesus will only bow down and worship him.

We may respond to this temptation: "But the world is the Lord's, and so are all the peoples and the kingdoms of this world!" This is, of course, the truth. God, the Creator and Ruler of all, is the true Lord of the whole universe, including this earth and its nations. But a battle has been ongoing ever since the fall. There is now a usurper, Satan, who calls himself the king of this world. He has set up an alternative kingdom over against the true king. So there is truth in what the devil declares to Jesus: Satan is (in a sense) the lord of this world. He lays claim to the world of human persons, for we are his because we are all sinners. This world in its rebellion against God is the kingdom of darkness. Those who do not worship God in true faith are indeed Satan's subjects. Satan is the ruler of this realm of disobedience. So he offers the nations of the world to Jesus—at a price.

All of us face such temptations. The hope is held out to us that there is a way for us to gain what we want by some other way, some easier way, than God's way of obedience and even suffering. But there is no easier way to be faithful to the Lord. There is suffering in following God's way because this is a fallen world in which Satan has power and in which our race is disobedient.

Satan and his forces, and his claim to rule over us, cannot be overcome by sheer force of might or by military victory. The only way to defeat the powers of darkness is by a completely different kind of power, the power of self-sacrificing love. Only by giving himself up to apparent defeat by Satan will Jesus be able to overthrow the devil's kingdom and set us sinners free from his dominion. That is why, once the disciples understand that he is the Christ, Jesus immediately speaks to them of the necessity of his suffering:

> From that time Jesus began to show his disciples that he must go to Jerusalem and suffer many things from the elders and chief priests and scribes, and be killed, and on the third day be raised. (Matt. 16:21)

Once Jesus has told the disciples of his own coming suffering, he then calls them to the same way of obedience:

> Then Jesus told his disciples, "If anyone would come after me, let him deny himself and take up his cross and follow me. For whoever would save his life will lose it, but whoever loses his life for my sake will find it. For what will it profit a man if he gains the whole world and forfeits his life?" (Matt. 16:24–26a)

On the occasion of his temptation, Jesus is offered the whole world by Satan. If he had accepted that offer and bowed down to worship Satan, then Jesus might have had a kind of power, but he would be a king alone, a king with no followers, no people who loved him. None of us would or could be saved; all of us would still be the subjects of the devil's kingdom forever, eternally bound in darkness. For Jesus and for us, there is no way to serve God, no way to overcome the devil, no way to inherit the world, except the way of worshiping God alone and following his call to obey him—no matter what the cost will be, no matter what sacrifice is required, no matter if life itself is lost.

Jesus' reply to the devil is what ours should always be:

> Be gone, Satan! For it is written, "You shall worship the Lord your God and him only shall you serve." (Matt. 4:10, quoting Deut. 6:13)

Jesus knows the first and greatest commandment, and he knows that it must never be set aside to gain his own desires or meet his goals, however great and good those goals may be. His calling is to worship God alone, to serve the Lord only, no matter where that takes him. Faithfulness to God is this simple, and this difficult!

This is our calling also, whatever we face in life, no matter how challenging it may be. Whatever trouble comes our way, whatever decision we have to make, our first response must always be: "I am to worship the Lord my God, and serve only him." This is the star that is to guide us every day of our lives, on every step of our way.

After Jesus has rebuked him, Satan leaves Jesus for a time. The Father, who, we may be sure, has watched this battle with joy in his Son's faith and righteousness, sends his angels to serve Jesus. In the same way, our heavenly Father, when we endure the tests that come our way with faithful obedience, is filled with delight and rejoices to give us his good gifts.

Satan will come to test us, and we, like Jesus, are to try to resist him. We must question our motives, knowing how easily we are deceived into justifying our own desires and wants. We must ask: "What is it that the Lord desires of me? What does Scripture teach me about what is pleasing to my heavenly Father?" Like Jesus, we must hide God's Word in our hearts so that we might be so aware of our motivations and so conscious of God's good will that we see right through the temptations that the devil, the world around us, and our own sinful natures thrust before us.

Yet even though our calling is to resist the devil so that he will flee from us, we must sorrowfully acknowledge that this is not who we are. We repeatedly yield to these temptations that Jesus resisted.

Thank God, we have a representative, a champion who has faced the devil's worst attacks and has won a great victory for us. Despite our failures in the face of temptation, the Father looks at us through his beloved Son, the One who has overcome the accuser for us. Because we are in Jesus, he looks on us with love. Because we are in Jesus, he does not count our faults against us. Because we are in Jesus, he forgives us. Because we are in Jesus, he lifts us up when we fall. Because we are in Jesus, he strengthens us for each day's struggles. Because we are in Jesus, the day is coming when he will give us complete victory over our enemy, and then we will never fail or fall again.

Questions for Reflection and Discussion

1. Which do you think would have been the most difficult of the three temptations for Jesus? Try to give reasons.

2. Can you think of other occasions in Jesus' life when he faced temptation? Which of the three temptations are these other occasions most like?

3. Which of these three types of temptation do you find most difficult to resist? Why?

4. How would you define your own greatest personal strengths, and what are your particular gifts? In what ways are these strengths and gifts also a source of temptation to you? How do your strengths become your weaknesses?

5. How do you deal with temptation when it comes? Try to think of some specific examples from your actual experience, both of having faithfully resisted temptation and of having succumbed to temptation.

6. In what areas in your life might you need to become less self-reliant and more dependent on the Lord? What steps will you take to yield your self-reliance to God?

7. How did you respond to the two stories about the young woman who threw herself off a tall building and about the young man with epilepsy who was told to no longer take his medication and to ignore medical advice? What might you say to the pastor of that young man if you were to meet him?

8. Have you ever put God to the test? What was the result?

In addition to praying about his coming death, Jesus prays about the impact of his teaching. He has spent much of the earlier part of the evening teaching his disciples. He has taught them about his coming death; about his going to be with the Father to prepare a place for them; about the promised coming of the Holy Spirit and the work the Spirit will do in the world, in the church, and in them. But again, Jesus does not assume that his evening of teaching will take root in his disciples' hearts. Rather, in this prayer he refers back to his teaching. He summarizes some of what he has taught and then prays that the Father will make the teaching effective, enable the disciples who have heard the teaching grow in understanding, sanctify the disciples with the truth, protect them from evil, and keep them in the faith.

We need to ask: "Who is this One who does not assume that his work and his teaching will be effective? Who is this One who acknowledges the need of the Father to ensure that his work and word will accomplish their purposes?" He is none other than the Son of God, the eternal second person of the Trinity, the Righteous One, the One who always does his Father's will.

The One who prays this prayer of humble dependence is not someone weak and disobedient to his Father's commandments—someone like you or me. The One who prays this prayer is not someone whose work is halfheartedly accomplished—someone like you or me. Nor is the One who prays this prayer someone whose work is done with mixed and confused motivations—someone like you or me. The One who prays this prayer is not someone whose teaching varies in its faithfulness and value—someone like you or me when we teach. Rather, the One who prays this prayer is Jesus. The One who prays this prayer is One whose teaching and work is always good, is always faithful, and is

---

9

Father, Glorify Your Name!

John 17:1–26

In our previous chapter, we saw Jesus being tempted by Satan to turn away from his calling, his commitment to serve the Father by going the way of the cross. Instead, the devil offered Jesus immediate glory and power. Jesus, however, chose a different kind of glory. He chose to reject the devil's way and to go the way of shame, the way of humiliation, the way of self-sacrifice, for he desired to serve and honor the Father in the way the Father willed. Our present chapter will pick up this theme of worshiping and serving the Father as he desires, for this is the heart of Jesus' great prayer recorded for us in John chapter 17. This prayer, as many readers will know, has since the early centuries of the church been designated Jesus' "High Priestly Prayer."

The study of this prayer of Jesus will bring us back to what is to be the central issue in all our prayers, expressed in the very first sentence of the Lord's Prayer:

Our Father in heaven, hallowed be your name.
(Matt. 6:9)

We are to pray that God's name will be hallowed, will be honored, and will be glorified in our lives. To further reflect on this theme, we turn to the prayer that Jesus prayed to the Father on the night before he died. Jesus' High Priestly Prayer marks the series of events on which all history turns. It is the prayer that comes at the end of Jesus' earthly ministry, at the end of his thirty-three years of life here in this world, at the end of his three years of serving, healing, and teaching:

> [Jesus] lifted up his eyes to heaven, and said, "Father, the hour has come; glorify your Son that the Son may glorify you, since you have given him authority over all flesh, to give eternal life to all whom you have given him. And this is eternal life, that they know you the only true God, and Jesus Christ whom you have sent. I glorified you on earth, having accomplished the work that you gave me to do. And now, Father, glorify me in your own presence with the glory that I had with you before the world existed." (John 17:1–5)

As this prayer of our Lord marks the end of his earthly ministry, it also marks the beginning of the most significant work ever accomplished in the history of this world. This work is, of course, Jesus' death on the cross and his resurrection. The cross and the resurrection together are the turning point in the history of humanity as a whole and the turning point in the life of each person. History for each of us, and for every other member of our race, stands or falls on how we respond to these events.

As we read the High Priestly Prayer, we see that Jesus' heart and mind are set on his coming arrest, trial, and

execution as a criminal. So this is a very personal pr[ayer] that Jesus prays. Yet even though his prayer is about [his] coming suffering and death, and about his particular [and] unique calling, the church has always also looked at J[esus'] prayer as a model for the prayers of all believers, as a so[urce] of instruction for our daily lives, and as a wonderful con[fort] in our times of personal need and trouble.

Jesus shows us many things by example in this pr[ayer,] of which the following are just a few: Jesus shows th[at we] are to live in dependence on his Father. He teaches us [that,] like him, we are to desire that his Father's name re[ceive] glory. Above all, he encourages us to know that we h[ave a] Great High Priest who is praying for us, asking tha[t our] heavenly Father will care for us in this world.

THE DEEPEST DEPENDENCE

The prayer might be summarized as an impo[rtant] step in Jesus' preparation for his coming crucifixio[n, for] in this prayer Jesus is dedicating himself to the Fath[er. He] does not simply go to the cross to die, assuming th[at his] work will be fruitful, assuming that his death will ac[com]plish the purchase of our lives and rescue many hu[ndreds] of millions of people from having to face the jud[gment] and anger of God—perhaps a billion Christian b[eliev]ers alive at just this particular time in history! R[ather,] Jesus sees the importance of praying that the Fath[er will] accept and be honored by his work of self-sacrific[e. The] High Priestly Prayer is an expansion of Jesus' pra[yer in] the garden of Gethsemane:

> Father, . . . not my will, but yours, be done. (Lu[ke] 22:42)

always true. This was so through all his years as a laborer at carpentry, when, we can be sure, he demonstrated the same dependence on his Father. And it was so in his years of public ministry.

Jesus is showing us in the clearest possible way that our work in God's kingdom will be ineffective without our prayer for the Father to accomplish his purposes through his blessing on all we do. He is showing us that our attempts to teach the Word will fail unless we pray that the Father send the Spirit to render them powerful and effective. As will our teaching of our own children at home, our teaching in our churches or any other kind of teaching ministry, our leading of worship, our music and our singing, our visiting, our serving, and our hospitality.

By the example of his High Priestly Prayer, Jesus is teaching us that in all the things we do, it is not enough to be busy for the Lord, not enough to be active in doing his work, not enough to be committed to teaching his Word. In addition to the work we do, we are always to beg the Lord to do his work in people's hearts and minds. For without his work, without his blessing, all our labors will be in vain.

This is why Acts records that the apostles devoted themselves to the ministry of the Word and prayer. In fact, the text reverses the order—the apostles said:

> We will devote ourselves to prayer and to the ministry of the word. (Acts 6:4)

Our ministry is to be prayer and the ministry of teaching; prayer and the ministry of serving; prayer and the ministry of music; prayer and the ministry of singing; prayer and the ministry of hospitality; prayer and the ministry of giving; prayer and the ministry of . . . You complete the sentence!

All of us, whatever our service to the Lord and to his people, are called to recognize that all our devotion and everything else we do will accomplish nothing unless we turn to the Lord in prayer, and unless the Lord blesses our efforts and establishes the labors of our hands.

Francis Schaeffer used to emphasize this point often. He would say that what we were all doing in the ministry of L'Abri, the ministry that he and his wife, Edith, had founded, was not just difficult for us; rather, it was impossible. This is true for any other ministry or for any church—indeed, for all work in God's kingdom. This is because all our work in any church, in any ministry, or in any family is about seeking to bring those who are not yet believers into a life of loving and trusting Jesus. All such work is also about seeing people grow in this life of love for Jesus, this life of delight in the truth of the Bible, and this life of glad obedience to God's commandments. This work is not just difficult, or even the most difficult work in the world—it is impossible.

Jesus himself made this very comment when he spoke of how hard it is for any wealthy person to enter God's kingdom, even harder than for a camel to go through the eye of a needle (these are very provocative words, for many of us are wealthy by the standards of most believers throughout history). The text then expresses how shocked the listeners were by Jesus' words:

> Those who heard it said, "Then who can be saved?" But [Jesus] said, "What is impossible with men is possible with God." (Luke 18:26–27)

The Schaeffers' reaction to this impossibility of their saving or changing anyone was to make prayer the very center of the work of L'Abri. One of Francis Schaeffer's favorite biblical images was of the church being pictured as the bride of Christ. He would say, in many different settings, that everything else in our Christian lives radiates out from our inner awareness of our being, individually and corporately, the bride of Christ. As his bride, we have as our calling to yield ourselves moment by moment to our Bridegroom, Christ, and to pray that as we offer ourselves to him, he would be pleased to bear his fruit through us.

The Schaeffers also wrote their conviction of the importance of this principle into the documents that govern the ongoing work of L'Abri Fellowship, their lifelong ministry, a work that has profoundly influenced the seminary where I teach and many churches and ministries all over the world: "We draw a distinction between men and women who are building the kingdom of God, and men and women who pray that God will build his kingdom and will be pleased to use their efforts as he does." They believed that there was a fundamental distinction, not a minor one, between Christian believers who seek to live in this reality and Christian believers who think it possible for them to build God's kingdom. Indeed, we may say that if we imagine that we are building God's kingdom for him, we will soon be trying to build our own kingdoms rather than the Lord's. As we read Jesus' prayer for the Father to bless his work, we must recognize that the Schaeffers were right about this.

For all of us, whatever our place of calling in society and our place of service in the church, it is not enough for us to be obedient to God. It is not enough for us to work hard and with integrity. It is not enough to apply ourselves to teach God's Word accurately and faithfully. Unless there is prayer as well as our faithful work in whatever job we do—prayer as well as our ministry (of whatever kind); prayer as well as the work of teaching; prayer as well as the work of worship; prayer as well as the work of counseling; prayer as well as the work of serving; prayer as well as the work of hospitality—no one will be truly blessed, no one will be changed, no one will believe, and no fruit will come from our labors.

Of course, God may choose to do his saving work despite our lack of prayer. But if that is the case, no thanks will be due to us; no praise will be given us from God; no "Well done, good and faithful servant" (Matt. 25:21, 23), will be spoken to us. No commendation or reward will be forthcoming from the Lord, no matter how intense our labors have been. We may say to him: "But I have done mighty works in your name; I have prophesied in your name! Does this not count for anything?" (This is a rough paraphrase of Jesus' words in Matthew 7:21–23.) If we did not do all things in dependence on the Lord, and to serve him, then all that God has accomplished, despite us, will count for nothing in terms of any truly pleasing and acceptable service to him.

Some reading this may ask: "Why is this? Why should we pray for God to make good work fruitful?" To reflect accurately on this, we must ask another question: "Why did Jesus pray that his heavenly Father would make his perfect work of offering himself up to death, and his perfect teaching, effective?"

The answer is simply that such prayer indicates a sense of humble dependence on the Father, a recognition that unless he works in the hearts of people, all our labors will be in vain. He is the Creator and Upholder of all things. He is the One who can make the light of truth shine into the mind. He is the One who can give life to the dead. He is the One who can woo the most obstinate person with his love. He is the One who can soften the hardest and most stubborn heart. In addition, simply to be human means to live a life of humility before the infinite and eternal God. Francis Schaeffer tried to express this in the following way: when anyone is saved, he or she must bow three times.

First, we must bow before God as the Creator and Sustainer of life. We are not self-created. We could not live for one moment apart from his holding all things together, and apart from his sustaining us in existence. We owe God life and breath and everything that we have and all that we enjoy every moment of our being. Coming to him, therefore, we are to bow to him and say: "You are God; I am not. I am utterly dependent on you."

Second, we must bow before God morally. He is the Lawgiver and Judge. He is the One whose character is the basis of our being able to say what is good and what is evil. We are not the source of law—he is. He is the One who, as our Creator, has the right to tell us how we are to live in obedience to his commandments. He is the One who has the right to call us to account before his judgment seat. He is the One who holds us guilty of breaking his laws, of not measuring up to his character, of falling short of his glory and of the glory for which we were made.

We must come to him, acknowledge that we are sinners dependent on his mercy, and confess to him that Christ has done for us, in his perfect life and in his sacrificial death, what we could never do for ourselves. Coming to him, therefore, we are to bow to him and say: "You are my Lawgiver and Judge. You are the Holy One. I have failed to keep your commandments and am bound in sin that I cannot control or overcome. Forgive me. Have mercy on me because of the blood of your Son shed on my behalf."

Third, we must bow before God in our knowledge. He is the One who is faithful and true, the same yesterday, today, and forever. He is the source of all truth: the light who lights every human being in this world, the fountain of all wisdom that comes to us and to all people in this world. Truth does not arise from us, but from him. Indeed, we have become enemies of God in our minds because of our evil behavior, and so we refuse to have truth in our knowledge. We are deeply ignorant, and we believe many foolish things in place of things that are evidently the truth. Coming to him, therefore, we are to bow to him and say: "Lord, you are my light and salvation. You are the true and faithful One. In you are hidden all the treasures of wisdom and knowledge. Forgive me for my ignorance, and for being so reluctant to come to acknowledge you as the truth. Thank you for opening my mind, and for enlightening the eyes of my understanding. Thank you for revealing your Son to me. Help me to grow in openness to your Word. In your light I will see light."

To be human, then, is to be dependent. That is why Christ, as the second Adam, as our faithful representative, prays for the Father to make his work effective. If Christ had this mentality of humble dependence as the true and perfect man, and as the eternal Son of God, how much more should we have this mentality of humble dependence? We who are weak and flawed in our humanity must seek to cultivate this prayerful dependence of our Savior. If you want the Lord to teach you the necessity of this, then ask him to teach you. He will!

Anyone who has been involved in ministry for any length of time will rapidly become aware how impossible is the work of saving and changing people. I remember a time when we had only recently graduated from seminary and had returned to L'Abri to work in the newly opened branch of the ministry in southern England. About a year after we had begun to serve in the work there, my wife and I were left in charge for the first time. On the second day I went upstairs to one of the men's bedrooms and discovered that a young man had tried to commit suicide. His wrists were slashed and blood was everywhere. He was as white as a sheet. I have to confess that I felt totally inadequate in this situation. Had seminary prepared me for this? What could I say to him? What could I do to make him believe that his life was worth living? How could I fix his problems? Of course, I could not, and I prayed in desperation: "Lord, help him. Lord, comfort him. Lord, give me the words to say. Lord, only you can fix any of this. I cannot. I need you. He needs you."

I will share another story. I was asked to go and speak for a conference on spiritual warfare at a church in Pennsylvania. The subject itself is challenging enough; but the evening before my flight from St. Louis I was driving one of my sons back toward our home, when we had an accident. It was the rush hour and we were driving against the flow of traffic, which was, of course, very heavy. The car fifty yards in front of me braked for a bend, and I responded by braking lightly. But my car spun around a couple of complete turns, went down a very steep bank over the side of the road, and came to rest, surrounded by trees, pointing back the way we had come—thankfully, exactly parallel to the road. If we had been pointing down, either front or back, we would have plunged down a slope at least a hundred feet to the bottom. Other cars stopped, and the slope was so steep that we needed a chain of human beings to pull us out of the car and up the slope. We opened the driver's door on the upside with great care, and both climbed out on that side, for we were afraid that at any moment the car would go all the way down. As I said, we were surrounded by trees, and it seemed extraordinary that we had hit none of them on the way down. Neither my son nor I, nor even the car, had so much as a scratch. When a tow truck came to pull us out, the driver said: "We will have to leave this till full daylight tomorrow, but someone up there was sure watching over you!"

As he took us home, our first response was one of over-whelming gratitude for our safety. My second response was to pray: "Lord, there must be some reason why the devil did not want me to speak at the conference this weekend. But Lord, you have work that you want to do there. Help me to do what pleases you this weekend. Watch over whoever it is that you desire to save." Later that evening I had to teach a community Bible study. I relayed the story of what had happened, and also told of my sense of Satan's desire to prevent me from going to the conference and my sense that God had something particular that he wished to do. I asked all those present to please remember to pray that the devil would be defeated that weekend, and that the Lord would do his work.

That weekend, after the second of my lectures on spiri-tual warfare, a woman came up to me and said, without any further introduction: "I am a witch, and I have been serving the devil." I knew, of course, that it was this woman whom Satan did not want me to meet, and this woman for whom the Lord had protected us so that I could meet her. After a conversation with her, I encouraged her to go to L'Abri. The accident, conference, and our meeting happened in November; the following March she went to the English L'Abri and became a believer in Christ.

I tell this story because it shows in a very graphic way how utterly dependent we are on God. No human person could have saved me and my son from a terribly tragic accident. No human person could have engineered such a meeting at just the right time. No human person could have saved someone who had given herself up to worship Satan and serve him. What is impossible for us, however, is possible for God!

Lest anyone conclude that I am suggesting that what we do is unimportant, I need to add that I have no such thought in my mind. It is not that we are to labor less diligently, whatever our work may be at home or on the job, in our ministry or in our churches. We are not, for example, to skimp the preparation for our teaching and just say, "God will do it!" It is not that we are to prepare the worship service with less care; it is not that we are to practice less at our music-writing, playing, or singing; it is not that we are to do shoddy service in the area of setting up the sound system or the taping, or the cleaning, or the organizing of the furniture's layout, or the serving of meals; nor is it that we are to neglect careful consideration of what a person says, or the necessity of having an open, listening, and discerning ear when we are talking to others one on one. I have written here primarily about ministry, but the point I am making is true of our labors in any area of life. In all of life we are called to two things: to labor faithfully, and to trust ourselves and the outcome of our labors to the Lord.

In all settings we are to recognize that we are to depend humbly on the Father, and we are to know that without his work, all our labors will accomplish nothing. This is our calling, this humble dependence on the Father every day of our lives to come.

> Unless the LORD builds the house,
>   those who build it labor in vain.
> Unless the LORD watches over the city,
>   the watchman stays awake in vain.

It is in vain that you rise up early
    and go late to rest,
eating the bread of anxious toil;
    for he gives to his beloved sleep. (Ps. 127:1–2)

This is a difficult lesson for us Americans to learn, for we have been taught to believe that life is what we make of it. We are persuaded that we are in control of our own lives and our own destinies. We believe that if we work hard, we can ensure a long life, a prosperous future, and our own happiness. But God's Word teaches us something quite different—and it is this something different, that we have been made to live in humble dependence on the Lord, that is Jesus' lesson to us in his High Priestly Prayer. And of course, this humble dependence is at the heart of all true prayer.

But the sad truth is that we do not do this well, just as we do not do anything else well. Paul's words in Romans chapter 7 about our not doing the good we long to do apply to us in the matter of humble prayer, just as they apply to every other part of our lives. When we reflect on our being made for a life lived before our Maker, we see with blinding clarity that a mentality of humble dependence is both essential and beautiful. But then, like the man who looks in the mirror, we go away and forget what we have seen.

Thankfully, the Lord is gracious and merciful. He knows that this is the way we are. He forgives us again and again, for none of us is constantly dependent on the Father in the way that Jesus was. We often find ourselves asking a week after some significant situation: "Lord, I forgot to ask you to bless my work. Please forgive me, and make the work effective anyway!"

154

HALLOWED BE YOUR NAME

At the beginning of John chapter 17, we see Jesus praying, "Father, glorify your Son that the Son may glorify you." He adds: "I glorified you on earth." Jesus' desire is that the Father's name be glorified in all he does. As we carefully look at Jesus' High Priestly Prayer, we will discover that it is similar to the Lord's Prayer in many ways. In fact, from the first centuries of the church, this prayer has been thought of as Jesus' own Lord's Prayer, for at its heart is Jesus' longing that the Father's name be hallowed.

The prayer is full of praise to the Father and of expressions that communicate a deep sense of the honor and respect that is due to the Father. Jesus calls the Father "Holy Father" (v. 11), "righteous Father" (v. 25), and the Father who loves (v. 23). All through the prayer Jesus speaks of the Father's work (vv. 2, 4, 6, 7, 8, 9, 11, 12, 15, 17, 18, 22, 23, 24, 25, 26). Many times he acknowledges all that the Father has done for him, all that the Father has done for us and for our salvation, and all that the Father will do for us in the future. Jesus is filled with humility before his Father, and his words overflow with the longing to honor his Father's name.

Another way to express this idea would be to say that in this John 17 prayer, Jesus models for us the lessons that he teaches us in the Lord's Prayer. As did Jesus, we should make this the heart of our prayers: love for the Father, praise for the Father, and longing for the Father's name to be glorified. In each of our lives at work, at home, at church—in our teaching, in our worship leading, in our singing and music, in our serving and giving, in our cleaning and hospitality, in our love for one another—in all we do in any part of our life, this is to be our passion: that the Father will be glorified in and through us.

Sometimes we come across lovely examples of a person who understands that this is what human life is intended to be. I was back in England a few years ago for a brief weekend of teaching, and I asked the young pastor, who met me at the airport in London, how he had become a committed Christian believer and how he had met his wife. He replied that there was one answer to my two questions, that both had taken place during his years in college at a particular meeting of a Christian student group. The visiting minister who was teaching for the evening asked: "What is the purpose of any of you being here at college?" Various students attempted answers, but then, my friend said, a young girl stood up and said something he had never heard before: "Our calling as students at this university is to glorify God and enjoy him forever." He said that he was amazed by her answer. He also noticed that she was very attractive!

This was the beginning of two life-changing events: his turning to the Lord and the first stages of his relationship with his wife-to-be. This also, of course, is the statement of the Westminster Shorter Catechism. This is our calling whether we are students in seminary, college, or school; whether we are at work; whether we are at home. For all of us, in whatever we do, this should be the central focus of all our prayers: "Lord, glorify your name in all we do."

When Jesus prayed this prayer, we know that the Father answered, "Yes!" When we pray this prayer about ourselves, about our work in the church, about our homes or workplaces, about any part of our daily lives, the Father will answer, "Yes!" For all of us, this is one prayer that we know will always be according to the Father's will. With complete confidence we can pray: "Father, glorify your name."

In an earlier chapter of these reflections on prayer, I gave the example of my father-in-law's service of firstfruits. The heart of his offering of his peaches was his desire that God would be glorified in everything he did, both as a farmer and as a servant of the living God. I want to encourage us all, once more, to design some formal ceremony like this, in our homes and in our workplaces—offering ourselves to the Lord, expressing our dependence on him, and asking him to glorify himself in all we do.

OUR GREAT HIGH PRIEST

We also learn from the John 17 prayer that Jesus is indeed our Great High Priest—hence the designation "High Priestly Prayer." Jesus is the One who stands before God the Father, as our substitute, as our representative, as our Mediator, as our Advocate. He is our Priest because he is the One who died for us. He is our Priest because he is the One who leads our worship whenever we come before our Father's throne to render to him praise, thanksgiving, confession, and offerings. He is our Priest because he is the One who prays for us.

Just as Jesus prayed for his disciples, the ones who were with him on the night of his prayer, so he also prayed for all of us who have believed through their word. He prayed for you and for me and for every other Christian believer on that night. But he did not pray for us just on that one night before he died. No, he prays for us now, at the Father's right hand. He always lives to intercede for us—this is the promise of the Word of God (Heb. 7:25).

The apostle Paul makes this same point in Romans chapter 8. Will Christ condemn us to the Father if we have trusted in him? Will he complain about us because we continue to struggle with our character flaws and personal weaknesses and areas of failing again and again? Will he look at us and lose heart when he sees our struggles, our inadequacies, and even our outright failures? Will he turn away and give up on us? Will he lose heart and say to the Father that he wants to forget about us, to wash his hands of us, to wipe our names out of his Book of Life? No! Christ stands continually at the Father's right hand and prays for us (Rom. 8:31–39).

If Jesus is praying for us (and indeed he is), then we may be sure that his Father hears his prayers and answers them. It is because Jesus always lives to intercede for us that we can have confidence that we will be saved completely. So as we read through John chapter 17, we need to know that every prayer Jesus prayed that night he is also praying for us, for you and for me, each day of our lives. If Christ is for us, who can be against us?

Questions for Reflection and Discussion

1. Does it surprise you that Jesus felt the need to pray that the Father would make his work and teaching effective? We might tend to assume that everything Jesus did was automatically effective because of who he was and how he did his work. Are you persuaded that it truly was necessary for Jesus to pray that the Father would bless his efforts?

2. How do you think about your own labors as a husband, wife, father, mother, friend, church member, or businessperson? Do you think of your work as needing

God's help to accomplish its full purposes? Write a brief prayer about your daily service of God, in which you express both your sense of having applied yourself to the labors of the day and also your sense of needing God's blessing on that work for it to be fully effective.

3. What do you think of Francis Schaeffer's statement: "We draw a distinction between men and women who are building the kingdom of God, and men and women who pray that God will build his kingdom and will be pleased to use their efforts as he does"? How would you apply this principle, first to your own life and then to your church?

4. What do you think of the early church's idea that this John 17 prayer is Jesus' personal Lord's Prayer?

5. How do you respond to Francis Schaeffer's idea that we all must bow three times when we come to the Lord?

6. Try to design a brief service for your home, your work-place, or your church that captures the spirit of my father-in-law's service of firstfruits on his farm.

7. Read John 17:1–26 again. What do you think Jesus meant by his words about glorifying the Father and being glorified himself (vv. 1–5)?

IO

JESUS PRAYS FOR GLORY

John 17:1–26

In the last chapter, we began to look at Jesus' High Priestly Prayer. We saw something quite beautiful there. In his prayer it is evident that Jesus does not depend on his own teaching abilities, but rather prays that the Father will cause his teaching to bear fruit in the lives of the disciples. In the same way, Jesus prays that the Father will make his coming death on the cross effective in the lives of those who follow him, and in the lives of all of us who come to faith in Jesus through their message.

In contrast to this mentality of Jesus, we so easily assume that if we do something well, it will automatically be effective in touching the lives of other people. But Jesus assures us that we need the Father's work for our work to bear its fruit. We find this lesson difficult to learn, and the reason for our stubborn independence must be the pride that was at the root of Adam and Eve's sin, which still lies at the core of our own sinful natures.

The most basic of all sins is seeking to live independently from God: to live pretending that we do not need him, to live as if we owned the world, to live as if we could make happen whatever we desire, to live as if we were in full control of our lives. Jesus, the last Adam, shows us another way, the way for which we were originally created, a way of dependence, of trust, of gladly accepting our finiteness and our need for the Father to do his work in and through us.

We also observed how Jesus modeled his prayer on the prayer he had taught the disciples, the prayer that we call the Lord's Prayer. Jesus prays that the Father's name will be hallowed; he prays about how he has accomplished the Father's will on earth; he prays for his disciples and for the whole church of the future to be protected from the evil one and to grow in truth and righteousness.

Particularly remarkable about Jesus' prayer is that he is facing the most difficult hours of his life: his soon-coming betrayal, arrest, and death. Yet he is thinking about others, about us! He prays that the Father's will may be done in our lives; he prays that we will be strengthened against temptation; and he prays that we might be able to resist evil.

PRAYER FOR OTHERS, NOT JUST FOR OURSELVES

This observation that Jesus prays for others even though he is facing terrible suffering that will come in just a few hours brings us to reflect on another aspect of the Lord's Prayer. The Lord's Prayer is a prayer not just for myself and my own needs; it is also a prayer for others. We are taught by Jesus to pray: "Our Father . . . . Give us . . . . Forgive us . . . . Lead us . . . ." (Matt. 6:9–13). Each petition is plural. Each of us is encouraged to know that we are one of our Father's many beloved children.

Yes, it is true that he loves me; yes, it is true that I am in need and that he encourages me to bring my needs to him. But I am not the only one he loves, and I am not the only one in need. Each one of us, whom he loves so dearly, is surrounded by others whom he loves as dearly. Each one of us who is in need is surrounded by others of his children in need. Our daily dependence on the physical and spiritual nourishment that our Father so generously gives to us in answer to our requests is the daily dependence of all the brothers and sisters in our families, in our churches, and around the world. When we pray, we are indeed encouraged to pray for ourselves, but we ought to pray not only for ourselves, but also for others.

What are our prayers like—yours and mine? Are they only, or primarily, for "me, myself, and I"? Or do we carry in our hearts a deep longing for others, both those whom we already know by name and some we do not yet know, but will one day meet? This is how Jesus prays to his Father and to our Father. He prays for himself, for his disciples whom he knows, and for countless others whom he has not yet met, most of them not even born and who would not be born for many centuries—such as you and me.

We need to model our prayers on both of the Lord's prayers, the prayer he taught and the prayer he prays, so that our prayers will be according to our Father's will. When we pray not only for ourselves but also for others, we recognize that we are part of our heavenly Father's family, part of the people for whom Jesus died, part of his beloved bride for whom he prays. When we pray not only for ourselves but also for others, then our heavenly

Father will be truly glorified when we pray. This, of course, should be our desire when we pray, just as this desire for the Father's name to be glorified is the central focus of Jesus' prayer.

GLORIFY YOUR SON

As we read this prayer, we see Jesus praying about "glory"—the Father's glory, his own glory, and our glory. The longing for glory is where his prayer begins, and glory is one of the central themes of the whole of this prayer to the Father:

> Father, the hour has come; glorify your Son that the Son may glorify you. (John 17:1)

> I glorified you on earth, having accomplished the work that you gave me to do. And now, Father, glorify me in your own presence with the glory that I had with you before the world existed. (vv. 4–5)

> All mine are yours, and yours are mine, and I am glorified in them. (v. 10)

> The glory that you have given me I have given to them . . . . (v. 22)

> Father, I desire that they also, whom you have given me, may be with me where I am, to see my glory that you have given me because you loved me before the foundation of the world. (v. 24)

What is glory? Glory is the unique magnificence, the particular honor, the special splendor of a person or thing. In the temptation narrative, we read that Jesus is shown "all the kingdoms of the world and their glory" (Matt. 4:8); and in the Sermon on the Mount, we read that "even Solomon in all his glory was not arrayed like one of these" (Matt. 6:29). Paul writes of the glory of the sun, moon, and stars, each of them having their own particular glory (1 Cor. 15:41).

Glory, then, is whatever it is that makes something unique, splendid, and beautiful. Every flower in this world, every bird, every creature, every sunset has its own particular glory because of the marvelous way in which God has made all things. Every person on this earth has his or her own personal and particular glory—those characteristics and gifts that set the person apart from all others—as well as the glory we all share and with which we are crowned because we are created in God's likeness to reflect his glory (Ps. 8:4–5). "Glory," we find, is used of the many parts and creatures of this world, and it is also used to describe us as God's image-bearers. Yet "glory" is primarily used to refer to God himself—and we see many examples in the psalms:

> The heavens declare the glory of God,
>> and the sky above proclaims his handiwork. (Ps.
>> 19:1)

> Lift up your heads, O gates!
>> And be lifted up, O ancient doors,
>> that the King of glory may come in.
> Who is this King of glory?
>> The Lord, strong and mighty,
>> the Lord, mighty in battle! . . .
> Who is this King of glory?
>> The Lord of hosts,
>> he is the King of glory! (Ps. 24:7–10)

Ascribe to the LORD, O heavenly beings,
  ascribe to the LORD glory and strength.
Ascribe to the LORD the glory due his name;
  worship the LORD in the splendor of [his] holiness.
    (Ps. 29:1–2; see also vv. 3–4, 9)

When we turn to the gospels, we see "glory" also used to describe what took place in the birth, life, and ministry of Jesus. We all are familiar with the glory mentioned at Jesus' birth—the glory of the Lord that shines all around the shepherds (Luke 2:9) and the "Glory to God in the highest" that is sung by the heavenly host (Luke 2:14). In John's account of the incarnation, he simply writes:

The Word became flesh and dwelt among us, and we have seen his glory, glory as of the only Son from the Father, full of grace and truth. (John 1:14)

John also tells us that Jesus "manifested his glory" whenever he did something miraculous—for example, in the turning of water into wine at the wedding in Cana (John 2:11)—and that Jesus revealed "the glory of God" when he raised Lazarus from his grave (John 11:40).

We may summarize in this way: the glory of Jesus as the One who is truly God was revealed in his birth, in his miracles, and in his whole life as he lived in obedience to the Father. Jesus' glory is also spoken of when he returns to reign on this earth. When he comes again, his glory will be seen not by his disciples alone, as at his first coming, but by the whole world (Matt. 16:27; 19:28; 24:30).

Then will appear in heaven the sign of the Son of Man, and then all the tribes of the earth will mourn, and

166

they will see the Son of Man coming on the clouds of heaven with power and great glory. (Matt. 24:30)

Glory, then, shows us the greatness, the wonder, the display of God's power in the life of Christ. So given this background to help us understand glory, how does Jesus speak about it as his life is about to come to an end?

THE GLORY OF ETERNITY

Jesus desires to share the same glory with the Father that he has had from before the creation of the universe and that is his with the Father through all eternity:

> Father, glorify me in your own presence with the glory that I had with you before the world existed. (John 17:5)

> My glory . . . you have given me because you loved me before the foundation of the world. (John 17:24)

This eternal glory is the glory of Christ's being fully God, the second person of the Trinity. This is the glory of everlasting fellowship within the Godhead, the glory of the love he has shared with the Father before anything else came into being. It is the glory of his power and majesty as the Designer and Creator of this vast and magnificent universe. It is the glory of the One who was immediately worshiped and adored by the multitude of angels and the great host of heaven when he called them into existence. This is the glory of his eternal being.

GLORY ON EARTH

Jesus prays about the way in which he has brought glory to the Father by his life and ministry here on earth:

I glorified you on earth, having accomplished the work
that you gave me to do. (John 17:4)

In everything Jesus did, he was accomplishing the
Father's will on earth: always speaking the words the Father
desired him to speak: always serving people as the Father
wished him to serve; always loving as the Father wanted
him to love; always keeping the Father's commandments
perfectly in everything that he did. In this way his whole
life is a glorious offering to the Father.

GLORY IN HIS DEATH

In addition to praying about his eternal glory as
God and the glory of his ministry on earth, Jesus also
prays: "Glorify your Son" (v. 1). Here Jesus is referring
to his imminent death on the cross. It is clear that Jesus
appears to think of his death as the supreme expression
of his glory.

What could be less glorious than death as a common
criminal? "Surely," we think, "his death was a shame, a
curse. Does not the apostle Paul describe the crucifixion that
way?" (Gal. 3:13). If you have seen the film *The Passion
of the Christ*, the terrible suffering that Jesus is depicted as
having endured seems far from glorious! John Calvin wrote
about this: "If it be objected that there never was anything
less glorious than the death of Christ which was then at
hand, I reply, that in that death we behold a magnificent
triumph which is concealed from . . . men."[1]

Why is Jesus' death on a cross the supreme manifestation of his glory? The answer to this question is found in
Jesus' words spoken a day or two earlier, during his final
week of teaching in the temple courts:

The hour has come for the Son of Man to be glorified.
Truly, truly, I say to you, unless a grain of wheat falls
into the earth and dies, it remains alone; but if it dies,
it bears much fruit. (John 12:23–24)

It is only by "dying" that a seed germinates to shoot up in
new life. In the same way, it is only by his dying that Christ
is able to bring life to the world. You and I—and all believers
throughout the earth, and throughout history—are the fruit of
Jesus' death. And how much fruit! Today, at this time in history,
about a billion Christian believers are spread across the nations
of this world, and at this present time, the church is growing
faster than at any other point in her history. In addition, countless numbers of believers are already with the Lord.

This is why Jesus' death is his greatest glory, his greatest
triumph, the most wonderful display of his eternal nature as
the God of love. Remember, the glory of something is its
most special attribute, the attribute that makes it uniquely
what it is. The cross reveals Christ's essential nature as One
who loves so deeply that he will sacrifice himself completely
for those he loves.

THE GLORY OF HIS PEOPLE

In this prayer, Jesus also prays about our glory:

All mine are yours, and yours are mine, and I am
glorified in them. (John 17:10)

The glory that you have given me I have given to
them . . . . (John 17:22)

Jesus makes the remarkable statement that he is glorified in us, and that he has given to us the glory that the

Father gave to him. His desire is that we might bring glory to him, and that his glory may be seen in us. Yet we read Paul's words that we "all have sinned and fall short of the glory of God" (Rom. 3:23), so we wonder: "How can Christ's glory be shown in us? We are so steeped in sin that it seems impossible that anyone could ever see us as revealing his glory." Just as with our question about the glory of Christ, the answer to this question about our glory is also found in the passage in John chapter 12, where Jesus speaks about the grain of wheat:

> The hour has come for the Son of Man to be glorified. Truly, truly, I say to you, unless a grain of wheat falls into the earth and dies, it remains alone; but if it dies, it bears much fruit. Whoever loves his life loses it, and whoever hates his life in this world will keep it for eternal life. If anyone serves me, he must follow me; and where I am, there will my servant be also. If anyone serves me, the Father will honor him. (John 12:23–26)

Christ's glory is made most clear in his death. Just so with you and me: glory is most fully made known in us when we imitate him, and when we are prepared to follow him wherever he goes. Jesus, of course, goes to the cross. He calls us to deny ourselves and to take up our cross. He is the Master, for all of us who serve him to obey; he is the Captain, for all of us who enlist with him to follow; he is the Pattern, for all of us who come to him to conform to. His life's essential mark is suffering, humiliation, and death. We are to follow him bearing the same mark. Christians are described in the book of Revelation as those who follow the Lamb wherever he goes (Rev. 14:4). That is why Jesus tells Peter that Peter will glorify God in his death

(John 21:19). Paul declares that his suffering brings glory to others (Eph. 3:13).

These are challenging words for us! What kind of glory are we seeking? The glory that is displayed on so many of our television programs—the glory of approval, of social status, of wealth, of beauty, of possessions, of intelligence, of fame, or even of having the neighbors from hell, and so getting our few moments of exposure for all the world to see?

Or are we eager to have the kind of glory that comes to those who follow Jesus, and who are therefore called to bear the mark of our Master? His glory will be revealed in us whenever we live in a way that is obedient to him, whenever our lives mirror his life of love and of service, whenever we speak the words of truth, of grace, of kindness that he desires from our lips. Each day we can then see touches of glory in our lives when we begin to do what delights him, and when we give ourselves to those things that bring blessing to the lives of others.

Most of all, however, glory is revealed in us when we are prepared to follow Christ by losing our lives in this world. When it is hard to be a Christian, when our lives are difficult and troubling, we are to regard such times as the very times when the Father is expressing most confidence in us—just as he did with Job. When we are experiencing tribulation, then we are told that the Father considers us worthy to follow in Jesus' footsteps, to be identified with him, to wear his badge of glory:

> Then they left . . . , rejoicing that they were counted worthy to suffer dishonor for the name. (Acts 5:41)

Such hard times may come to us in many ways: in grief and bereavement and being alone; in sickness and disability;

in financial hardship and demanding schedules; in difficult people to love and to serve; in pressure and trouble that arises because of our faith and because of our commitment to be obedient to the Lord. In all our hard times, whenever life is difficult, the devil desires to undermine our faith, to cause us to doubt the Lord, and to become bitter and angry about our lot. But the Lord's desire in such times is that we pray that we might glorify him in our troubles.

I will share a family example—this one about our sister-in-law. She died just a few years ago after struggling with Lou Gehrig's disease for about eight years. This is the disease that afflicts the great physicist Stephen Hawking. The disease gradually spreads to the whole body, atrophying all the muscles, so that movement becomes impossible. Usually Lou Gehrig's begins with the hands and feet and eventually progresses to the lungs so that the person cannot breathe. With our sister-in-law, the disease started with her lungs and then worked its way outward to her extremities, and so it killed her more speedily than is usual. Because she was a physician herself, she knew exactly what was happening to her, and how the disease would gradually take over her whole body.

For the last two or three years, eating was very difficult and she could not speak—but she could communicate by tapping out notes to us all on her computer. What was remarkable about her was her lack of bitterness and self-pity. She continued to serve people in need as long as she could, and to the end she continued to be concerned about others.

I wrote to her once to tell her what an inspiration she was to all who knew her. She replied that she had prayed that the Lord would help her not to become bitter, that he would help her to continue to serve and glorify him in her life right till the end, and that he would enable her to continue to care for others in every way she could. As her body wasted away, her inner nature was daily renewed by the Lord until the very close of her life. We visited her to say goodbye a few days before she had her feeding tube removed. After our time together she wrote me one last e-mail, just one sentence spelled out with great difficulty, one hand dragging the other over her keyboard: "When do I get my glorified body?" She already had a spirit greatly glorified, a life in which Christ was revealing his glory.

When we see a surgeon perform a truly difficult operation, we honor him for the "glory" of his work. When we see a beautiful piece of art or hear wonderful music, we honor the artist for the labor poured out in the creation and performance of the work. So with us, the more difficult our life, the more confidence God is showing in us, and the greater the glory. The way in which we are a blessing to others is the way of the cross, for this is the way that Jesus has brought his blessing to us (Col. 1:24).

In talking about suffering to those who worked with her, Amy Carmichael used to use the image of an opal to communicate this truth. It is the flaws at the heart of the opal that cause the precious stone to reveal flashes of light and radiate color. So it is with us: as we experience tribulation, and yet continue to trust Christ and to serve him and to serve others in love, so his light and radiance are revealed in us. C. S. Lewis, the author of the Narnia stories, and of the science fiction novel *Perelandra*, has as the central theme of these books that self-sacrificing love is the greatest power in the universe. This is also true in J. R. R. Tolkien's *Lord of the Rings*. This is the glory of Christ, and this is to be our glory also. There is no greater glory in the kingdom of God than the way of the suffering servant.

Future Glory

There does remain for us a glory of a different kind, and Jesus also prays about this other glory:

> Father, I desire that they also, whom you have given me, may be with me where I am, to see my glory that you have given me because you loved me before the foundation of the world. (John 17:24)

We will, one day, see the glory of Jesus in his heavenly kingdom. This is his longing for us, that we might be with him and see our Lord no longer in his humiliation, but in his glory as the One who shares love and majesty with the Father through all eternity. Each one of us who puts our trust in Jesus, however weakly and inadequately, will see him in his eternal glory. We will see him as the apostle John saw him in his vision on the Isle of Patmos:

> Then I turned to see the voice that was speaking to me, and on turning I saw seven golden lampstands, and in the midst of the lampstands one like a son of man, clothed with a long robe and with a golden sash around his chest. The hairs of his head were white, like white wool, like snow. His eyes were like a flame of fire, his feet were like burnished bronze, refined in a furnace, and his voice was like the roar of many waters. In his right hand he held seven stars, from his mouth came a sharp two-edged sword, and his face was like the sun shining in full strength. (Rev. 1:12–16)

We will see him and be able to bear that vision, for we will share his glory. We will be renewed by him, perfected in righteousness, and we will be given our own glorious resurrected bodies. When that time comes, we will experience the glory of being fully free from sin and from all the troubles of this world.

Questions for Reflection and Discussion

1. What to you is the most precious aspect of the High Priestly Prayer of Jesus?

2. As you think about your own prayers, what proportion of them reflect the "Our Father" of the Lord's Prayer, rather than simply "My Father"? How will you start to look outward to others a little more in your prayers?

3. "Glory" means the unique splendor of a thing or a person. What do you consider to be the glory of spring, or the glory of winter, or the glory of some other aspect of creation that you particularly take delight in?

4. As you think about Christ's three years of ministry (apart from his death), what do you consider to be the special glory of his ministry?

5. As you think about the church in which you are a member, what do you consider to be the particular glory of your church?

6. What about you? What is your special glory? You may wish to answer this one just between you and the Lord.

7. Do you find it difficult to think of Jesus' death as his supreme manifestation of glory?

8. Do you know any Christians in whom you see the "suffering servant" kind of glory made known? Why is this so special, and how do you see their beauty shown?

9. Do you have favorite books in which the glory of being a servant ready to sacrifice oneself is a central theme?

II

JESUS PRAYS FOR HIS PEOPLE

John 17:1–26

In the last chapter, we saw that in his High Priestly Prayer, Jesus was preparing for the climactic events of his life on earth that would take place in the next few hours: his betrayal by Judas, his arrest, the trials, and his execution as a criminal. He prayed that these appalling events would be the ultimate revelation of his glory, for they would show in human history the reality of love that has existed within the Godhead from everlasting to everlasting. His unjust betrayal, trial, conviction, and execution—even though they were carried out by his human and demonic enemies—were, in truth, taking place according to the explicit will of God, as the apostle Peter declares in his sermon on the day of Pentecost:

> This Jesus, delivered up according to the definite plan and foreknowledge of God, you crucified and killed by the hands of lawless men. (Acts 2:23)

Jesus sacrificed himself, in obedience to the Father's will, in order that we, who deserve death, might have eternal life. This is why his death is the fullest expression of his glory.

In addition to praying that he would be glorified by the Father in his death, Jesus was thinking not just about himself, but also about us. He prayed for the disciples who were there with him, and for all who would come to faith in him. He prayed that our lives would bring glory to the Father, just as his life did. He prayed, too, that we might enjoy his eternal glory. He is our Great High Priest who is praying for us every day, asking that the Father's name may be glorified in our lives.

As we read Jesus' prayer for us, we can glimpse what Jesus thinks is most important for us in our Christian lives. He is shortly to die, but because the purpose of his death is our salvation, as he prays for his death, he prays with us on his mind. We are told in Hebrews that Christ is always praying for us:

> He holds his priesthood permanently, because he con-
> tinues forever. Consequently, he is able to save to the
> uttermost those who draw near to God through him,
> since he always lives to make intercession for them.
> (Heb. 7:24–25)

If we ask, "What does Jesus pray for us now, as he intercedes for us at the Father's right hand?" we can answer the question with confidence by looking at Jesus' prayer for us on the night before he died. It is clear that the most urgent needs for our lives are the ones that are most deeply imprinted on his heart as he faces his death on our behalf. What are these concerns for us that led him to pour out his prayers for us to the Father?

1. Jesus prays that we might be kept in the Father's name, just as Jesus kept his disciples, and that we might be protected from the evil one (John 17:11, 12, 15).
2. He prays that we might have the full measure of his joy within us (v. 13).
3. He prays that we might be sanctified by the truth of the Father's Word as we go out into the world, just as Jesus himself was in the world (vv. 14–19).
4. He prays that we might be with him and see his glory (v. 24).
5. He prays that we might be one (vv. 11, 20–26).

The first four of these prayers of Jesus for us will be considered in this chapter and the fifth in chapter 12. We can learn from these petitions what we should consider to be of most importance in our daily lives. We ought to regularly ask ourselves: "Are these five issues on the heart of Jesus the issues that are on my heart?" "Are these the longings for my life that fill my own prayers?"

Before we look in more detail at these five petitions, a couple of general points need to be made about obedience and protection.

A CHALLENGE

Jesus prays about our need to be obedient to God's commandments, and he prays about our responsibility to be in the world. Christians are not to retreat from the world of sin and unbelief, nor are we to separate ourselves from unbelievers. Rather, we are sent into the world just as Jesus was sent into the world. He delighted in being with sinners, for that is why he came. In turn, sinners were delighted to be with him. It is in the challenging context of people who do not know God, who do not love Jesus, and who do not obey the laws of God that the Christian is called to live a life of love for God and walk in obedience to his law. Our life is not to be one of separation from unbelievers and of retreat from the world, but one of love for the world and love for sinners—in imitation of Christ.

THE FATHER'S HELP

Jesus prays that the Father will protect us from the evil one as we go out into the world in obedience to his wishes. Fear of the devil sometimes causes Christians to retreat from the world. We think we will be safer if we spend as much time as possible with fellow believers and as little time as possible with unbelievers. Jesus urges us not to fear the devil (Luke 12:4–7), but rather to fear God and do what he says. If we do what God tells us, and that is "Go into the world," we may be sure that Jesus is praying for our protection. God promises that he will care for us if we do what he says. We might even say that Christians will be safer if we are in the world, where God wants us to be, than we will be if we retreat from it. We will be safer if we are with unbelievers in obedience to the call of Christ! If we obey him, we can be confident that he is praying for us, for we will be right where he wants us to be, and we will need the help that he is eager to give.

PROTECTION FROM THE EVIL ONE

The first petition that Jesus prays for us in his High Priestly Prayer is that we might be protected by the power of the Father's name from the evil one (John 17:11, 12, 15). Sometime that same evening in which he prayed this prayer, Jesus told Peter that Satan desired to have him, that he might sift Peter like wheat (Luke 22:31). We may presume that Satan also has the same desire to sift each of us like wheat. In his first epistle, Peter teaches us that our adversary the devil goes around like a raging lion, wishing to devour us and to destroy our faith (1 Peter 5:8).

We may ask the question: "Will we know for sure when the devil is sifting us and when he is seeking to devour us?" In an earlier chapter, we saw that we have no infallible knowledge about such things, for we cannot draw back the veil that separates the seen and unseen worlds. If we read the book of Job, we are informed that Satan is behind Job's troubles. Yet Job is never told this. He must struggle without knowledge of just why such disasters befall him. He must walk by faith, rather than by sight. Job must entrust himself to the One he knows to be just and good in all that he does—though, of course, Job's faith is sorely tested.

Like Job, we are not usually aware of precisely what the devil is doing to bring disruption to our lives, for nowhere does the Scripture promise us sure knowledge about such matters. This does not mean, however, that we can ignore the devil's plans against us. We are assured by Scripture that he will attack us. That is why Jesus prays for us against the devil, and that is why Peter tells us that Satan is seeking to devour us. From Paul we know that as a normal part of the Christian life, we will be battling against Satan and his servants:

> For we do not wrestle against flesh and blood, but against the rulers, against the authorities, against the cosmic powers over this present darkness, against the spiritual forces of evil in the heavenly places. (Eph. 6:12)

Because this wrestling against spiritual forces of wickedness is part of ordinary Christian experience, we are called to resist the devil and to stand firm against his attacks. Paul urges us to "take up the whole armor of God" against this assault upon us (v. 13). In particular, he reminds us that with "the shield of faith" we can "extinguish all the flaming darts of the evil one" (v. 16).

We cannot claim with certainty that every one of our sufferings and hardships is the devil's work, for there are many sources of troubles in this world: our own sins, the sins of others, the hostility of the world, the brokenness of our universe because of the curse, the Lord's discipline. But even though we cannot with confidence accuse the devil of being the source of all our troubles, we can be sure no matter what the source that Satan will be actively using our sorrows to discourage us and to undermine our faith. He is always going around like a lion to devour us. He is always lying, accusing, and murdering. This is his nature, and his purpose is to seek to tear us away from our security in Christ. Therefore, we must always pray against him, no matter what the source of our particular sorrows.

In addition, there will be times when we may suspect that especially difficult troubles that come upon us are indeed a result of Satan's direct attacks on us. We know that his passionate longing is to overcome the good work that the Lord is doing in our lives and through us. So when we see the Lord at work in our lives in very powerful ways, we can assume that the evil one is not pleased.

The seminary where I teach has seen an unusual cluster of severe medical problems among the members of our faculty. We all suspect that Satan has a hand in this because God has been building his kingdom on our campus, with great power, these past few years. We may suspect that these health troubles are Satan's work, but the veil or curtain between the seen and unseen world is not drawn back. Even when we are not sure whether particular difficulties are a direct consequence of the devil's hatred of us as God's people, however, we can be sure that in all our difficulties the devil desires to turn us away from the worship, trust, and service of God. Consequently, we must be aware of the devil's purposes against each one of us, so that we might echo Jesus' prayer for us with the words of the Lord's Prayer every day: "Deliver us from the evil one!"

Even more than seeking refuge in our own prayers, we should take heart because Jesus lives to intercede for us. Just as he prayed for Peter that his faith would not fail despite Satan's desire to sift him like wheat, so he is praying for us that our faith might not fail. He is also praying that the Father will keep us in his name (that is, by his power) from the evil one's power. It is a great comfort to know that Jesus, who was so severely tested by the devil, is praying for our protection. It is also a great comfort to know that Jesus has already mastered and defeated Satan at Calvary. This casting down of the devil by Jesus' death is another aspect of the glory of the cross.

THE FULL MEASURE OF HIS JOY

Second, Jesus prays to the Father that we might have the full measure of his joy within ourselves: "But now I am coming to you, and these things I speak in the world, that they might have my joy fulfilled in themselves" (John 17:13). (The NIV states: ". . . so that they may have the full measure of my joy within them.")

Jesus knows that for us to be able to endure the constant troubles and sufferings of this life, we need a full measure of the Father's joy. Jesus himself was able to endure the cross and despise its shame because of the joy that the Father promised him and held before him (Heb. 12:2). This is to be our longing and prayer also, that our Father would grant us joy no matter what difficulties we face. Remember the example I used in an earlier chapter of our friend who is paralyzed from the neck down—he is a man full of joy. Or think of the story I told of my sister-in-law struggling with Lou Gehrig's disease—she spent her last couple of years with an extraordinary courage, contentment, and even joy. My mother-in-law cared for Dad while his mind gradually disappeared as he was overcome by dementia. She said to us, even in the midst of the daily challenge of looking after a man who could no longer respond to her most of the time: "I don't think I have ever been happier."

This past year my wife and I have been listening to a dear friend who discovered that her husband had been unfaithful: first becoming addicted to pornography, then visiting strip clubs, and finally paying for sex with prostitutes. Of course, she has been devastated, and she has spent days in misery, hardly able to speak. Yet God has given her joy even in the midst of such unspeakable pain. Jesus' prayer for this joy in our lives is his reminder, and his promise to us, of the Father's commitment to care for us. His delight is to give us a full measure of his joy, for he knows the pains we must bear here in this world.

This prayer for joy reflects Jesus' desire for us that despite the pressures, anxieties, and problems of this life, we might have a deep sense of joy in knowing him, just as he had a deep sense of joy in knowing the Father. He prays for the full measure of joy for us—not a little joy, or a scant measure, but a full measure.

This raises many questions for us: "Is this full measure of joy what we experience as we reflect on our lives?" "Is this full measure of joy what we expect or even hope for?" "Do we, in fact, pray for a full measure of joy?" "Do we believe that such joy is possible?"

There are all kinds of difficult issues here. Often, perhaps, we are satisfied with something far less than a full measure of joy. Maybe we don't even want joy. Perhaps we desire personal fulfillment and happiness instead—fulfillment and happiness as we define them, or rather fulfillment and happiness as our culture defines them for us: comfort, financial security, a good job, a nice home, a decent car (or two or three), moderately up-to-date clothes of good cut and quality, a beautiful wife or handsome husband, healthy and gifted children . . . you complete your list of what you think might make you happy and fulfilled. Even though many of these things are good things, however, they are not what the Lord promises us, nor are they what Jesus requests for us. The central questions here are: "What is it that I long for?" "How do I define my deepest happiness and fulfillment?" "What will I give my life to pursue?" See, for example, Paul's words in 1 Timothy chapter 6, where he warns us that the desire to be rich is a trap that plunges men into all kinds of ruin and destruction, and even causes us to wander away from the faith (1 Tim. 6:9–10).

What are our priorities for life? Perhaps we can root out the fundamental issue by asking the question this way: Imagine if someone were to ask our children, "What do your parents desire for your lives; what are the goals for your lives that are most important to them?" How would our children reply? Would they say: "Well, I think that my parents are eager for me to be successful; they are always pushing me to get excellent grades; they want me to look good; they are anxious for me to get into one of the best colleges; they are longing for me to get a well-paying job"?

Of course, nothing is wrong with any of these goals. But if they are our priorities for our children, then they have become our idols. Such idols are, in themselves, good, for they are good gifts of creation. But even if we desire God's good gifts more than anything else, our goals are still too small. Job has some lovely words to say about this:

> If I have put my trust in gold
>   or said to pure gold, "You are my security,"
> if I have rejoiced over my great wealth,
>   the fortune my hands had gained,
> if I have regarded the sun in its radiance
>   or the moon moving in splendor,
> so that my heart was secretly enticed
>   and my hand offered them a kiss of homage,
> then these also would be sins to be judged,
>   for I would have been unfaithful to God on high.
>   (Job 31:24–28 NIV)

The Lord wants to give us his joy, not just more personal and material pleasure—though he does indeed give us many personal and material pleasures for our enjoyment because he loves to give his children good gifts (see 1 Tim. 6:17–19). Jesus prays for a full measure of his joy for us, and he urges us to pray the same prayer. His desire for us is that we will have joy: joy that will endure through sickness and health, poverty and wealth, and all the other vicissitudes of life.

What is joy? It is not easy to define, but we can make a beginning by setting out some of the aspects of joy according to the Scriptures. Joy includes a deep contentment in knowing the truth; a thankful and glad awareness that we are loved by the Lord; a happy amazement that we are forgiven and accepted by him; a pleased and glad recognition that this is his world; a delight in receiving the good gifts that come to us daily from his hand; an eager anticipation of the bliss of the life to come—because we long with aching hearts for all our tears to be wiped away and our sorrows removed forever.

Part of joy is the knowledge that one day the troubles that bring such sadness to our lives will all be gone. This raises for us the issue of depression, or melancholy, as it used to be called. Most of us know people who struggle all through life with depression, which can sometimes be very severe.

Some of the most gifted and accomplished men and women in history have had to live with a deep sense of melancholy about life. Abraham Lincoln was one. (For an excellent article about how his acute and abiding sadness was a factor in the outstanding job Lincoln did as president during one of the most troubled times in our history as a nation, see Joshua Wolf Shenk, "Lincoln's Great Depression," *The Atlantic* [October 2005].) Winston Churchill was another—he called his bouts with depression "the black dog." One of the greatest American poets of the twentieth century, Sylvia Plath, struggled with severe depression all through her life. Among Christian leaders, the great poet and hymn-writer William Cowper endured terrifying periods of melancholy. Francis Schaeffer was also one who had regular bouts of depression.

We have now learned that a genetic predisposition can be involved in such sadness, and that cases of chemical imbalance can be helped with medication. As I write this, I have just been speaking with a dear friend, one of our graduates who serves with an inner-city youth ministry, in which he has been greatly blessed by the Lord. He has wrestled with severe melancholy all his life and has recently been prescribed medication by his psychiatrist, a fellow believer. This medication has transformed his life from "night to day," to use his own words.

In the Scriptures, too, we read of God's people going through times of sadness and even desperation. See, for example, the account of Job's suffering and misery (to say that Job was depressed risks severe understatement!); or the record of Elijah's anxiety and sorrow that led to his wishing to give up life (1 Kings 19); or Paul's moving and encouraging words in 2 Corinthians chapter 1 of his troubles that left him "so utterly burdened beyond . . . strength" that he almost "despaired of life itself" (2 Cor. 1:8). Paul declares that his suffering was far beyond his ability to endure and that in his heart he felt the sentence of death.

It is important to notice that Scripture nowhere accuses those who go through such times of great sorrow of being lacking in faith or unspiritual. Jesus himself told his disciples that his "soul [was] very sorrowful, even to death" (Matt. 26:38), and he asked Peter, James, and John to stay awake and watch with him, for he needed encouragement from his dearest friends. They were so sorrowful at his sorrow that they fell asleep (Luke 22:45). We have already noted the words of Hebrews 12:2, which tell us that "for the joy that was set before him" Jesus endured the cross. His fullness of joy would come only after his death. This is true, of course, for all of us—we look forward to an everlasting joy that will be beyond all comparing with the temporary and transient joys we experience in this life.

You are probably asking: "But what about the joy in *this* life for which Jesus prays? And what about the command of Paul that tells us that we are to rejoice always?"

(Phil. 4:4). These questions have no simple answers. Some Christian believers find joy much easier to experience than others: some because our lives have been much less troubled than the lives of others; some because we were born with a more cheerful disposition; some because the Lord grants us particular seasons of joy that can almost overwhelm us with unspeakable happiness. And some believers endure very difficult lives; others are born with a melancholy temperament or even with severe mental illness; still others, again, may be asked by the Lord to endure by faith times of very great sadness. We should note, in regard to this diversity of our experience, the account in Hebrews chapter 11 of the differing challenges that believers must face in this life. Yet despite these vast differences of life situation, all are called to live by faith, and all are to recognize that their full reward lies in the life to come. For every single believer there will be joy unspeakable for all eternity. For now, in this stage of life, we are encouraged by Jesus to pray for joy, and also to seek, like Paul, to learn the secret of being content whatever our circumstances (Phil. 4:11–13).

SANCTIFICATION BY THE TRUTH

The third element in Jesus' prayer for us is that we might be sanctified by the truth of the Father's Word as we go out to serve him in the world, just as Jesus himself was in the world (John 17:14–19). For us all, the beginning of growth is the recognition that we need help to deal with the challenges of sin, for we do not cope well either with our own sinful dispositions or with the pressures of the broken and idolatrous cultures in which we live. We even lack understanding of human life—without God's account of what life is truly meant to be, what its problems are, and how we have been designed to live. So where do we turn to find help for understanding and a description of our calling for life? Jesus understands that the Father has given us his Word to be our help, our guide, our source of direction, our challenge, and our comfort, so that we might walk in righteousness. The psalmist prays:

> How can a young man [or any other person] keep
> his way pure?
> By guarding it according to your word.
> With my whole heart I seek you;
> let me not wander from your commandments!
> I have stored up your word in my heart,
> that I might not sin against you.
> Blessed are you, O LORD;
> teach me your statutes!
> With my lips I declare
> all the rules of your mouth.
> In the way of your testimonies I delight
> as much as in all riches.
> I will meditate on your precepts
> and fix my eyes on your ways.
> I will delight in your statutes;
> I will not forget your word. (Ps. 119:9–16)

This needs to be our regular prayer, just as it is Jesus' prayer for us—though the psalmist's recommendation as to how we are to approach our daily life is a way to think that is rather different from the way we usually think, and it is very far removed from what popular culture is teaching us through the media. Jesus describes as "blessed" those who hunger and thirst for righteousness, and he promises that if we do have such a hunger, we will be satisfied (Matt. 5:6). The words from the psalm quoted above challenge us to have this same hunger (see also Pss. 1, 19).

But we live in a cultural setting that urges us to hunger for just about anything other than righteousness, and not one of us finds it easy to resist this pressure. This is why the "prosperity gospel" is such a popular message, even though it is so clearly contrary to biblical teaching. And this is why many of us who are committed to faith in Christ, even though we reject the prosperity gospel, pray most of our prayers about the health, wealth, and happiness of ourselves and of our own immediate families and close friends.

I stress once more that it is not wrong to pray such prayers, for the Lord loves to give his children good gifts. But we do need to ask ourselves two questions: "What is the predominant theme of personal prayer in the Scriptures?" and "What is the predominant theme of our prayers?" The first question must be answered by acknowledging that the predominant theme of prayer in God's Word is the desire for living in submission to God's laws and being obedient to his will. The Lord wants us to hunger and thirst for righteousness, and to cry out for the Holy Spirit to aid us in our calling to see the kingdom come in our lives. Our answers to the second question will challenge us to reorient our prayers away from our cultural obsession with personal happiness and towards God's passion for us to walk in his ways.

What will be the consequence if we do start to pray with serious intent that we might be sanctified by the truth, and if we do begin to treasure God's commandments more than wealth, comfort, and success, and if we do try to set our passions on true righteousness? If we conform our prayers and the priorities of our lives to God's will for us—our sanctification—we will enjoy a much deeper and richer satisfaction in our daily lives than we have ever experienced. Indeed, along with a growing passion for righteousness, we will find that the joy that Jesus asks for us will find a resting place in our hearts.

BEING WITH JESUS AND SEEING HIS GLORY

Fourth, Jesus prays that we might be with him and that we might see his glory (John 17:24). Jesus himself lived in the confident hope of entering his Father's presence and of sharing with him the glory they had enjoyed together through all eternity. Earlier that same evening he had taught his disciples that in his Father's house there are many rooms, and that he was going to the Father to prepare a place for them. He also said that he would come back to get them and take them to himself so that they would be with him where he is with the Father (John 14:2-3).

Here in his prayer for us Jesus prays that all of us who believe in him will get to share that same glory that he enjoys eternally with the Father. This is the hope we live with—that Jesus' glory will be ours, and that it will be ours for all eternity to come. That is why Paul is able to say without any exaggeration that beyond all comparison to our present "light momentary affliction," we look forward to an "eternal weight of glory" (2 Cor. 4:17). We are to live in this expectation, seeing what is unseen now, and praying that we might have the hope of this glorious future rooted deep within our hearts.

This is a difficult, even unwelcome, teaching for us. You might disagree with my words here, and even be shocked by them, but I chose these words with great care. Both the secular culture around us and the culture of our churches teach us that we have hope in this life, that here and now we can have happiness, defined as the right to pursue life, liberty, prosperity, and personal fulfillment. We begin to believe that we have the right to expect that we will have long life, good health into old age, fulfilling work and career, financial comfort and security. We spend most of our time in prayer asking for these things, things that are in fact the widely held assumptions, expectations, and hopes of our culture. But we need to understand that this is not where Scripture encourages us to put our hope. Paul writes:

> If in this life only we have hoped in Christ, we are of all people most to be pitied. (1 Cor. 15:19)

> We look not to the things that are seen but to the things that are unseen. For the things that are seen are transient, but the things that are unseen are eternal. (2 Cor. 4:18)

John Calvin makes a remarkable comment on the promise of Paul: "Honor your father and mother . . . , that it may go well with you and that you may live long in the land" (Eph. 6:2–3, quoting Ex. 20:12). Calvin asks: "Why would anyone imagine that long life in this world should be desired?"[1] His words seem almost incomprehensible to those of us who live in the Western world today. We must remember, however, that Calvin was writing in a time when the death of children, the death of women in childbirth, and death through sicknesses that we can now easily cure were commonplace. All these things and many more, including almost constant war in Europe, were part of everyone's life expectation. In Calvin's time, Christians knew that their hope was in the future life. We need to rekindle this hope and to pray that we might learn to set our hope on the life to come that Jesus has promised us.

Questions for Reflection and Discussion

1. Are you persuaded by the provocative idea about our calling to the world: that we will be safer in the world among unbelievers than if we live a life of retreat and separation, because that is where Jesus wants us to be? How can you take courage in Jesus' prayers for us as we seek to be in the world as he was in the world?

2. Have you ever sensed that you have been under particular attack from the devil? What was your response?

3. What I had to say about our priorities in this life is very challenging. Where do you think your priorities and goals might need to be changed?

4. If you have children, what do you think they would say are your goals for them? For all of us, what might others (e.g., people in our workplace) say are the goals and central pursuits and passions of our lives?

5. Have there been times in your life when you have experienced a deep measure of joy?

6. Many Christians struggle with depression. Is this true for you, for members of your family, or for close friends? How do you seek to be a support and comfort to those who often feel overwhelmed by the sorrows

of life, or who tend to have a melancholy attitude about themselves?

7. As you look at the list of five issues in our lives for which Jesus prays in his High Priestly Prayer, are you surprised by the things he includes and the things he leaves out? Recall that as he faces death, his mind and heart are concentrated on those things he considers to be most significant for us.

8. As you think about your prayers, do their central concerns match with Jesus' prayers for you, or are they very different? How do you think your prayer concerns should change?

12

JESUS PRAYS FOR UNITY

John 17:1–26

I will treat in a chapter of its own Jesus' final petition for us in his High Priestly Prayer. This is his prayer for unity among those who believe in him, his prayer that we might be one (John 17:11, 20-26). Our unity is of the utmost importance to the Lord, for he prays this petition for us repeatedly. We need to notice how many times he prays that we might be one and that we might live in the love of the Father and the Son (vv. 11, 21, 22, 23, 24, 26). This is quite clearly the biggest burden on his heart for us his people as he is about to die. His foremost passion for us is that we might be united, so he prays for this over and over again. We will look at this prayer for unity and for love among us in some detail, but first we need to see all his words about this subject set out before our eyes:

> And I am no longer in the world, but they are in the world, and I am coming to you. Holy Father, keep

them in your name, which you have given me, that they may be one, even as we are one. (John 17:11)

I do not ask for these only, but also for those who will believe in me through their word, that they may all be one, just as you, Father, are in me, and I in you, that they also may be in us, so that the world may believe that you have sent me. The glory that you have given me I have given to them, that they may be one even as we are one, I in them and you in me, that they may become perfectly one, so that the world may know that you sent me and loved them even as you loved me. Father, I desire that they also, whom you have given me, may be with me where I am, to see my glory that you have given me because you loved me before the foundation of the world. . . . I made known to them your name, and I will continue to make it known, that the love with which you have loved me may be in them, and I in them. (John 17:20–26)

Who Cares about Unity?

Jesus prays that we might be one. We live in such an individualistic culture that this does not seem of particular importance to us. Our goals, as the sociologist Robert Bellah tells us, are vivid personal feelings and personal success;[1] but to Jesus our oneness is of much greater significance. Yet this is problematic for us, alien to the way our culture shapes us to think. So as soon as we raise the subject of unity, Christians seem to feel the need to make qualifications, rather than to wrestle with what Jesus has to say to us about being one with fellow believers. We try to identify the people with whom we don't need to be one, rather than getting on with the calling to be one. Christians even use this text as the basis for a battle cry against any kind of ecumenical unity! Instead of turning the text into a battle-ground of defining those excluded from oneness, we need to submissively sit at Jesus' feet and listen to his heart for unity among us. In our reflecting on this topic, perhaps a series of questions will help us.

UNITY—WITH WHOM?

For whom does Jesus pray that they might be one? He prays for his disciples (those who are already his followers when he offers up his prayer), and also for all those who would believe through their teaching. In other words, Jesus prays for oneness for the whole believing church. We are called to unity with all other Christian believers, regardless of denominational affiliation, educational background, social or economic status, language, national origin, or race. If someone is truly a Christian, then we must strive to realize the oneness with that person for whom Jesus prays.

Jesus, of course, knew that in the world there would never be true unity, for in the world there will always be divisions, fights, wars, and rumors of wars. Jesus himself teaches as much in his Olivet Discourse (see Matt. 24:6-8). The downside of fallen human persons is aggression, pride, envy, and bitterness, and these characteristics alienate us from one another. This is the sad history of our world. We see every form of alienation around us every day, between individuals, between groups, and between nations.

Among us as Christians, however, it is to be different! We are to be one. The divisions between people—divisions that began at the fall in the garden of Eden, and then spread out to impact all human relationships—are to begin to be overcome in those who belong to Christ. But how is this to be realized? That brings us to another section of this prayer for believers to be one.

THE BASIS FOR UNITY

On what basis does Jesus pray for our unity? Jesus does not pray that we might somehow begin to be one, but rather that we might continue to be one. He prays that we might realize the unity that is already ours. We already possess it because we are kept in the Father's name, because the Father, by his power, has already bound us to Christ in faith. Because we are united to Christ by the Father, we are also united to each other.

Jesus longs for us to see ourselves as already united to all other believers by Christ. We share the same faith, of course, but it is more than this. Each Christian is my brother or sister for whom Christ died. It is said that blood is thicker than water; well, we are bound together by the blood of Christ. We have one heavenly Father, so we are truly members of one family. We have the same Spirit indwelling all of us. We have been washed with the same water of baptism. We share in the same communal meal of celebration of Christ's work on our behalf. All believers are bound together by God and by the gospel.

Paul addresses this issue in his letter to the Ephesians. He declares that once we were separated from Christ, but that now our relationship with God and with other people has been transformed:

> Remember that you were at that time separated from Christ, alienated from the commonwealth of Israel and strangers to the covenants of promise, having no hope and without God in the world. But now in Christ Jesus you who once were far off have been brought near by

the blood of Christ. For he himself is our peace, who has made us both one and has broken down in his flesh the dividing wall of hostility by abolishing the law of commandments and ordinances, that he might create in himself one new man in place of the two, so making peace, and might reconcile us both to God in one body through the cross, thereby killing the hostility. (Eph. 2:12-16)

Paul is referring, of course, to Jews and Gentiles who have been made "one new man" in the church through Christ's death—but he himself makes it clear that this peacemaking and reconciling work of the cross is true for all divisions that exist between people (see 1 Cor. 12:12-13; Gal. 3:28-29; Col. 3:11-15). In these passages Paul applies his words about our unity in Christ to all cultural, economic, gender, and racial divisions, along with the divide of religious, dietary, and ritual practices that kept Jews and Gentiles apart. We should take note of the number and strength of Paul's expressions in the Ephesians 2 passage quoted above: "you who once were far off . . . brought near"; "he himself is our peace"; "made us both one"; "has broken down . . . the dividing wall of hostility"; "abolishing the [religious, ritual, and dietary commandments]"; "create in himself one new man in place of the two"; "so making peace"; "might reconcile us both to God in one body through the cross"; "thereby [by the cross] killing the hostility."

The very heart of Paul's words about unity is that bringing his people together is central to the purpose for which Christ died on the cross. Unity with fellow believers is not an optional extra for the Christian. It is as I am joined in one body with others that we are together reconciled to God. Another way to express Paul's point would be to say that if

I am not reconciled to others, then I am not reconciled to God himself. We cannot tear apart what Christ has joined together by his death. His intent in going to the cross was that in this one offering of himself, he would overcome two fundamental human problems: our alienation from God and our alienation from each other.

We need to ask ourselves what divisions and hostilities between people are part of our lives, both as churches and as individuals. Jesus charges us to pray about these matters and to find our unity in knowing him. In heaven we will be part of a great throng of believers drawn from every tribe and tongue and people and nation. This multiracial and multicultural unity will be a joy to us. We should be practicing for heaven now, tuning ourselves in the present life for this great united yet multivaried concert!

The great English pastor and poet John Donne wrote about his own preparation for heaven using this marvelous image of being an instrument in a great chorus, an instrument being tuned now for the life to come:

> Since I am coming to that holy room,
> Where with Thy choir of saints forevermore,
> I shall be made Thy Music, as I come
> I tune the instrument here at the door,
> And what I must do then, think now before.

"Hymn to God, My God, in My Sickness," lines 1–5

Jesus desires that our lives be a preparation for our future perfect unity with all fellow believers. So he prays that we might understand now this future unity that will be ours completely, and that we might practice now what he has already purchased for us. Jesus prays: "Let them be brought to complete unity!" He does not want this to remain merely an interesting idea for us to think about. He does not want us to consider this as a possible addition to the Christian life: "If I have some spare time in my busy schedule, then I will try to build in some quality unity; perhaps I might just be able to fit in an hour for unity this coming week!"

Rather, the Lord wants us to understand that we have been granted unity as a basic part of our new life in Christ, and that we are to be dedicated to realizing that unity, just as we are to be dedicated to obeying his commandments about financial integrity, sexual purity, marital fidelity, loving our children, or serving only him.

It is a contradiction to think of a solitary Christian, just as it is a contradiction to think of a Christian who has no sense of sin or of the need to become more righteous. It is also a contradiction to think of racially prejudiced Christians, or of Christians separated by social class, by economic status, or by the kind of church they attend.

THE UNITY OF THE TRINITY

We need to think more deeply about what kind of unity Jesus prays for. How complete is the unity that our Lord desires us to have? If we set down his words, we will see that Jesus prays for a very high level of unity for his people. He prays:

> that they may be one, even as we are one. (John 17:11)

> that they may all be one, just as you, Father, are in me, and I in you, that they also may be in us . . . . (v. 21)

203

that they may be one even as we are one, I in them and you in me, that they may become perfectly one . . . .
(vv. 22–23)

that the love with which you have loved me [from before the foundation of the world] may be in them, and I in them. (v. 26; see also v. 24)

Our unity is to reflect the unity of the Trinity, the unity of the Father, Son, and Holy Spirit. Jesus does not mean that we are to become part of God—that is, that we are to be absorbed into God like a candle flame lost in the overpowering brightness of the sun. Nor does he mean that we are to lose our identity in each other, or in some faceless Christian mass—the church as "mashed potatoes," as one preacher used to express this idea!

The Son and the Father are one, but the Son is distinct from the Father. In the same way, we are to be one with fellow believers but are to keep our distinctiveness. It is like a good marriage. A husband and wife may become truly one. Yet as they do become one, their different genders, personalities, and gifts are not crushed, but rather flourish. This is most obvious in sexual union, where the differences of being male and female are most apparent, yet there is the deepest consummation of unity. This should be true in all other areas of married life as well. My desire has always been to encourage my wife's gifts of music and of fluency in the French language in every way I can, so that they develop and come to full fruition. These are gifts that I do not possess, but I know that I am enriched by Vicki's gifts, not threatened by them.

In the same way in the church, where there is true unity there will be encouragement of the differences of race, of culture, of personality, of calling, and of gifts, and the mutual delight in this diversity should bring about an even deeper sense of unity and of love for one another. One of my personal great comforts is that I serve at a seminary where our relationship as faculty has a deep level of realized unity. There is no pressure to conform to some stereotype of what a professor should be; instead, there is a delight in the uniqueness of each person and a powerful commitment to unity, to love, and to thinking more highly of each other than of oneself.

Within the Trinity these commitments are perfectly realized. The Father, the Son, and the Spirit have a perfect unity, a perfect love for each other, a complete desire to bring glory and honor to each other. This last point is a key to the realization of unity. If we are self-centered, seeking our own glory and honor, thinking only about our own comfort, security, and needs, pursuing our individual happiness, then there will be no unity with fellow believers. Instead, we will bite and devour each other. Just think of the destructive nature of gossip! But if we are committed to having the mind of Christ, that is, to being intentional about thinking of others more highly than we think of ourselves, then unity can be welcomed and enjoyed. In Philippians Paul addresses this question:

> So if there is any encouragement in Christ, any com-
> fort from love, any participation in the Spirit, any
> affection and sympathy, complete my joy by being of
> the same mind, having the same love, being in full
> accord and of one mind. Do nothing from rivalry or
> conceit, but in humility count others more significant
> than yourselves. (Phil. 2:1–3)

Here is one simple way to put this concept: "Humble people get on well together." This is true in marriage, in the family, in friendship, and in the church. Humility before one another, along with a readiness to serve one another faithfully, so that we might give pleasure, honor, and fulfillment to the other—these are at the heart of all true unity.

HOW IS UNITY REALIZED?

How does Jesus pray that this unity will be achieved? We have begun to answer this question in what was said about humility, service, and honor, but Jesus adds something else for us. It is by his abiding in us, and by our abiding in him, that we will begin to experience unity more and more. He prays that "they also may be in us" (John 17:21); he prays that "I [might be] in them and you in me" (v. 23); and he prays: "I will continue to make [your name] known [to them], that the love with which you have loved me may be in them . . . " (v. 26). Jesus and the Father (and the Spirit, too; see John 14:17) have committed themselves to us to dwell in our hearts. The Trinity comes to dwell in us, that they might enable us to be one with the Godhead and one with other Christians. As we reflect on this triune presence within us, and as we recognize that same presence in one another, so we will move toward a greater sense of unity: "This is indeed my brother or my sister for whom Jesus died; this is my brother or my sister in whom the Father, the Son, and the Holy Spirit dwell! The triune God who loves me and who dwells within me moves me to unity with all those in whom he makes his home."

Jesus prays that we might abide in him, that we might trust him, that we might love him, and that we might ask him to fill our hearts with his love for each other. What is impossible for us is possible for him! He has already given to us the glory that the Father gave him (John 17:22). What is this glory that he has shared with us? It is the mentality of being a servant, the readiness to live a life of self-sacrificing love. This is the glory of Christ, and he has shared this glory with us. This is the glory of the Trinity—this commitment to honor, to love, and to service.

This triune God has come to dwell in us and to call us to share in the same kind of life that has forever characterized the members of the Trinity. Father, Son, and Spirit make their home in us, that we might become more and more like the persons of the Trinity, that we might become people devoted to honor, love, and service, and that we might thus experience a little of the unity that the persons of the Godhead eternally enjoy.

WHAT IS THE PURPOSE OF OUR UNITY?

For what purpose are we to demonstrate this unity? We might answer this question by saying that our unity will glorify the Lord, or that it will bring joy to our own hearts and lives. These are, of course, true answers to the question; but Jesus emphasizes another purpose when he prays for our unity:

> so that the world may believe that you have sent me. (v. 21)

> so that the world may know that you sent me and loved them even as you loved me. (v. 23)

Jesus desires that we be one so that the world may believe that the Father sent the Son. He prays for our unity so that the world will know the Father's love. One of the most powerful weapons of the Spirit to bring people to faith in Christ is the reality of love demonstrated in the lives of Christians.

I became a Christian when I was in college largely through seeing the beauty of a life of love and humble service in one of my fellow students (I have written at length about the impact of Michael Tymchak on my life in *The Heart of Evangelism*[2]). All through my life I have been most impacted by lives that display a reality of love, and it is the same with our impact on the lives of others.

God delights to use quite unselfconscious expressions of love in our lives. When we were buying a car, my wife and I had arranged to meet at the dealership. The salesman was so moved by the obvious affection and love between us that the Lord used this simple and very genuine display of delight in our seeing each other to help bring him back to a life of faith in and obedience to Christ, as well as bringing me a lifelong friend. I think, too, of a couple beginning to attend our church. When I asked the husband why they were coming, he replied: "We have never seen a community like this, and we want to become part of it." Repeatedly it was our experience in L'Abri that many unbelievers who came to stay at the branches began to think seriously about the Christian faith, and eventually came to faith in Christ, in response to the reality of love in the lives of those who worked in that ministry. All churches in which people are regularly being converted can make this same testimony. Many who become believers are moved by the quality of love and unity that they see in the lives of church members.

Francis Schaeffer used to describe love as "the final apologetic" of the Christian. We can talk about Jesus' love in dying for us until the world ends—and we should talk about his love, his death, his resurrection, and all the other wonderful truths of the gospel until the world ends. But non-Christians need to *see* the love of God in Christ at work in the lives of believers. Why should anyone believe what we say about the love of God for sinners if they do not see love for one another in our lives and for other sinners like ourselves? Jesus longs for us to demonstrate unity and to give ourselves in love for one another. Why? Because he has a heart for the world of sinners. Of course he does! That is why he came into this world. That is why he died. That is why he rose again. That is also why he was petitioning the Father for our unity in his High Priestly Prayer on the night before he died.

Questions for Reflection and Discussion

1. How important has unity between Christians been for you? Would you say that it has been a major emphasis of your life, or of the teaching of your church?

2. As you have thought about unity, where has your focus been? Has it been on issues of denominational affiliation, on issues of class or race, or on something else? All of these are, of course, important areas in which we should work for unity with one another.

3. In what areas do you think you need to start praying for unity with other believers in your own life?

4. Do Christians who are different from you have reason to believe that you are working at realizing unity with them?

5. What excuses have you used to postpone working at unity with other Christians? Why are these excuses inadequate?

6. Do you give unbelievers who look at your life reason to say, "It is amazing how those Christians love one another"?

7. Do you know any people who have become Christians because of the love they saw among Christians?

8. Are there any who have become believers at least partly because of the love they have seen in your life?

Appendix A

AN ESSAY ON MYSTICISM AND PRAYER

When we think about the nature of God as he has revealed himself, we are overwhelmed with a sense of his glory and power. Even when we look at the beauty of his creation, we find ourselves struggling to find words to express the wonder of what we see. We cling to great words of poetry that set out for us what we feel inadequate to declare. All of us have loved hymns, poems, and biblical passages that say for us what we want to say. And this makes us thankful for the imaginative gifts that God has given to particular people. C. S. Lewis wrote that Psalm 19 is one of the greatest lyric poems in any language. Many believers delight in that psalm, which celebrates the glory of God revealed in the heavens, and which employs the image of the sun in its radiance being like a bridegroom rejoicing in the consummation of his marriage, or like an athlete delighting in his speed. One of the psalms that I cherish is the eighth psalm:

> O LORD, our Lord,
>   how majestic is your name in all the earth!
> You have set your glory above the heavens. (Ps. 8:1)

If we find ourselves struggling for words when we look at the wonder of what the Lord has made, how much more will we struggle for words when we try to express the glory of God himself! Again, we find ourselves turning to the words of a hymn, a poem, or a beloved section of Scripture. It is no surprise that many Christians turn to the worship songs in the book of Revelation or to the book of Isaiah, using the words we find in those Scriptures when we want to praise God or when we try to set down what we think of the Lord.

The songs in Revelation lift us up to heaven, for they set out for us, in words matching the feelings in our hearts, the joy that we cannot find words to express. In like manner, Isaiah was a great poet; consequently, we find passages such as Isaiah chapter 40 a great comfort and inspiration, with his statements of God's tender care and yet of his incredible power and greatness, and also his repeated questions from the Lord:

> To whom then will you compare me,
>   that I should be like him? says the Holy One. (Isa.
>   40:25)

Later in his book, we find Isaiah writing once again about the unmatched glory of God, about how far beyond our thoughts and imaginations is the Lord:

> For my thoughts are not your thoughts,
>   neither are your ways my ways, declares the LORD.
> For as the heavens are higher than the earth,
>   so are my ways higher than your ways
>   and my thoughts than your thoughts. (Isa.
>   55:8–9)

> For thus says the One who is high and lifted up,
>   who inhabits eternity, whose name is Holy:

"I dwell in the high and holy place,
  and also with him who is of a contrite and lowly
    spirit,
to revive the spirit of the lowly,
  and to revive the heart of the contrite." (Isa.
    57:15)

One very wonderful aspect of biblical truth is expressed here by Isaiah: the Lord is far above us and our imaginings—yet he delights to make himself known to us, and to be in fellowship with us, when we humble ourselves before him. He is high and lifted up, but his joy is to dwell with the lowly.

The more we understand any aspect of biblical truth, the more we should be filled with the mystery and wonder of it. The better we see the extraordinary love of God for us in Jesus Christ, the deeper should be our sense of awe and inexpressible gratitude for the amazing grace of God. The more clearly we see God, the more we will be humbled and overcome with reverence. This is why our hearts are so moved that tears spring to our eyes when we hear the words of John as he describes his vision of Christ in Revelation chapter 1, or when we listen to his account of the scene that dazzled his senses when he looked through the door into heaven and saw the throne of God and the Lamb surrounded by the cherubim, the elders, and the multitude of angels adoring him (Rev. 4, 5).

Mystery and wonder are a necessary and completely appropriate response to God's revelation of himself. Awe at the transcendent glory of God should be part of all our worship: in our readings, our hymns, our music, our prayers, and our proclamation of the Word. Many of the most deeply loved hymns capture something of this response of mystery, awe, and wonder before God's infinite and eternal majesty. Some of my favorites are the hymns on the resurrection written by John of Damascus in the eighth century, and other hymns from the ancient church, such as "Be Thou My Vision" (Irish, eighth century), "Jesus, the Very Thought of Thee" (Latin, eleventh century), "Jesus, Thou Joy of Loving Hearts" (Bernard of Clairvaux, ca. 1150). Many of J. S. Bach's chorales contain a lovely combination of words, which fill us with joy and wonder, and of music, which ravishes the heart.

Every age of the church produces musical offerings and hymns that lift us up to heaven. Today, contemporary writers and composers, such as Stuart Townend and Keith Getty, give us this union of the mystery of the truth of the gospel of Christ and music that matches the words, bringing both gladness and tears into our hearts and eyes (just two examples of their work are "The Power of the Cross" and "In Christ Alone").

This appropriate sense of the glory, wonder, and mystery of God and of the gospel of Christ has led believers throughout the history of the church to reflect on what this means for prayer. Much of this reflection has been greatly helpful to the devotion of Christians for many generations; this is true also for so many of the prayers written down for the blessing, encouragement, and edification of other believers. The aim of this essay is to answer the following question: "What are the appropriate limits to this kind of reflection?" In particular we will look at the tradition of mystical spirituality and to try to hold some of its teachings up to the light of Scripture.

THE CHALLENGE OF MYSTICAL TEACHING

When we start reading or listening to teaching about prayer, we face some particular challenges. One is that ideas and practices from the tradition of mystical spirituality often find their way into reflections on the subject of prayer. You might respond: "What is wrong with that? Some beautiful writings have come from the mystical tradition in the history of the church, so why should there be a problem?" Or you might say: "I have Christian friends who find great help in the writings of the Christian mystics—are you criticizing my friends?" And some of you might be thinking: "But I find the writings of the mystics helpful myself, and using their works has enriched my own prayer life."

These are important points and questions to consider. I want to begin my comments about mysticism with the glad acknowledgment that many genuine Christian believers are deeply influenced by the mystical tradition of spirituality. I also gladly acknowledge that many of the great Christian mystics—both in the Eastern church and in the Western church—were true believers in Christ. My desire is not to try to discredit anyone's faith in Christ, nor is my desire to attack anyone.

Rather, I wish to ask some foundational questions: "What are the basic teachings of mysticism?" and "Where do these basic teachings come from?" We then need to go a little further and ask whether these basic teachings of the mystical tradition conform with basic biblical teaching. We will seek to answer the question: "Does this basic teaching of mysticism accord with biblical teaching about the nature of God, about the nature of ourselves as human persons, about the nature of our human dilemma, and about the nature of the salvation that God has won for us in Jesus Christ?"

These reflections are necessary, for at many times in the history of the church God's people have been influenced by the mystical approach to spirituality and particularly by the mystics' understanding of contemplative or meditative prayer.

You may say: "But this is a good thing!" If we desire to be faithful to God's Word, however, we should be prepared to ask the question: "Is the mystic's understanding of contemplative or meditative prayer truly in accord with biblical teaching?"

DEFINITION—WHAT IS MYSTICISM?

To answer this question of definition, I will begin with the words of two authors who have written extensively on the mystical tradition in the Christian church. Both of these writers are sympathetic to this tradition and are seeking to give a positive view of the teaching and practice of the mystics.

Georgia Harkness defines mysticism in this way: "The belief that the human spirit, finite, limited and clouded though it is, can nevertheless experience the presence of the Divine Reality which undergirds and permeates the world."[1] Evelyn Underhill writes of the mystic's goal as union with the absolute: "The mystic's goal is union with the Absolute."[2]

The mystic stresses not the five senses, but the individual's soul or "religious receptor" as the highest source of the knowledge of God; the mystic regards the internal and immediate experience of God as the most direct and convincing source of knowing God.

What is the impact of this approach on Christians who embrace the mystical tradition? The Christian mystic tends to stress the "inner light," the "internal word," or the "Spirit within" more than, or at least alongside, the Scriptures as the source of true knowledge of God. The Christian mystic is likely to say that the Scripture gives him or her knowledge about God, but that the internal soul gives direct and therefore more compelling personal knowledge, or experience, of God. This understanding of the importance of the soul as the primary means of knowing God is part of a way of seeing the world. Such a view does not stand by itself, but rather goes with a set of presuppositions, or assumptions, about the nature of reality and about the relationship of us as human persons to that reality.

What are these presuppositions? How does the mystic see the world and our life as human persons within the world? How does the mystic speak about God? What does the mystic think about how we come to know God? What kind of knowledge of God is possible for us as human beings?

Presuppositions of Mysticism

1. Our five senses and our minds are not the only means of approach to knowledge or to human living, for the material world is not the only world.

2. A realm of spirit exists that is related to, though not identical with, the material world, and this realm of spirit is within us as well as above us. This realm of spirit may be called by various names, depending on the religious tradition in which the mystic stands: the Absolute; the Ground of Being; Ultimate Reality; the Universal Self; the One; God. Whatever this realm or reality is called, this "One" is considered as being above and beyond this visible world. The Christian mystic will call this One "God"; the Muslim mystic will call the One "Allah"; the Hindu mystic will call the One "Brahma"; the Buddhist mystic will call the One the "Sacred" or "Holy." (I should add here that there are so many differing approaches within what is called Buddhism that it is probably not appropriate to summarize in this way. On a popular religious level, some of these approaches are atheistic; some acknowledge many divine beings; some are more pantheistic. On a philosophical level,

217

all such discussions and distinctions concerning the final nature of reality are only preliminary, for it is claimed that the experience of existence and the pretensions of knowledge are themselves aberrations—the only ultimate reality is the enigmatic Nirvana or "nonbeing" ["nirvana" means literally "to be extinguished"].)

3. The human spirit is part of this realm of spirit and so can discern some kinds of truth without ordinary sensations or rational thoughts, but rather directly—through spiritual insight, through intuition, through visions or dreams. Such directly perceived truth and knowledge is the most important, precious, and dependable form of truth available to us.

4. The human spirit can have communion with this One, either in momentary ecstasy or in a steadier and more enduring sense of Presence.

5. This communion with the One may lead to purity of life. Christian mystics always have this emphasis because they have one foot firmly grounded in Scripture. Even with Christian mystics, however, as Georgia Harkness says, "the mystics stress moral purity and the need of penitence, but because of the divine element within man as basic to his nature, they have usually taken a less bleak view of the human soul."[3]

These basic assumptions of the mystic about reality lead to our next area of exploration. Given these presuppositions about "God" and about the way in which human persons know "God," what will this worldview mean for the way mystical experience is understood?

Marks of the Mystic's Experience

1. Ineffable: Mystical experience is indefinable in language; no language can express what the mystic experiences,

so the mystic is mute. Nothing can be said, for in himself or herself the mystic finds feelings, or a state of being, rather than concepts. "The mystic mind says this and that, gyrating around the unutterable abyss."[4]

2. Noetic: This is the term used in the mystical tradition in a similar sense to that of Plotinus. "Noetic" means literally "knowledge of the intellect," so "supernoetic" or even "antinoetic" might be a more accurate term. What is meant here is that mystical experience is insight into depths of truth that cannot be reached by the mind or the intellect.

3. Transient: Mystical experience is usually brief and fleeting. Because intense emotional energy must be expended to enter into a mystical experience, to maintain a mystical state for long periods might well be psychologically damaging.[5]

4. Passive: The quieting of the mind and the emotions is necessary to experience the voice and presence of God. But here "passive" does not mean that one does nothing; rather, this passive receptivity requires intense effort and disciplined practice to maintain.

5. Ecstatic: One must stand outside of oneself. Mystical experience requires the emptying of oneself, withdrawing for a while from the normal self and from normal life in the external world. Such withdrawal from oneself is necessary to contemplate the divine.

It should be evident as we reflect on these five points that some of their ideas do not immediately strike a chord with biblical teaching. The Scriptures call us to "be still, and know that I am God" (Ps. 46:10); to deny ourselves (Matt. 16:24); and to acknowledge that God says, "My thoughts are not your thoughts, neither are your ways my ways" (Isa. 55:8). They also describe John after his vision of the glorified Christ in this way: "When I saw him, I fell at his feet as though dead" (Rev. 1:17).

One could add other passages to the brief selection above, in particular the accounts of Ezekiel's and Daniel's visions, other visionary sections of the book of Revelation, and Paul's description of his being caught up into the third heaven. But it is far from clear that the experiences described in these verses are to be understood in the same way as the experiences sought and described by the mystic.

That leads to this question: "If mystical experience and understanding is not clearly taught in Scripture, how and when did these ideas and approaches come into the thinking and practice of parts of the Christian church?"

MYSTICISM'S ENTRY INTO THE CHRISTIAN CHURCH

Plotinus

The systematic entry of mysticism into the early church goes back to Plotinus, a third-century philosopher who was a Neoplatonist rather than a Christian. His ideas were very influential on many Christian thinkers—the great Augustine, for example, called some of his teaching "gold from Egypt."

Plotinus wrote of a Trinity, not in the Christian sense of three equal and coexisting persons in the One God, but rather as deriving from each other in a kind of chain of being. These three he described as:

1. The One; the Source—Plotinus did not think of this One as a personal being.

2. The Nous or Mind—this sphere of eternal thought forms, ideas, or organizing principles exists without past or future in an eternal Now.
3. The Psyche or Soul or Oversoul—this is the principle of creative energy: through it the eternal world exists.

From these three we descend by degrees through a chain of being to encompass all of reality. For Plotinus, the eternal world is linked with the world of time and space, for it generates all life.

- From the Soul comes the soul of human persons.
- From the soul of human persons comes the body.
- Matter has no reality of its own, but is a transient state, though because it comes from the soul it shows traces of the divine.
- Matter, physical life, is the source of evil, though matter is not wholly evil.

We should notice how very different these teachings of Plotinus are from a truly biblical understanding. We can think of the following few examples taken from a biblical worldview: of the triune God as three eternal persons in the One God; of human persons as physical/spiritual beings who are the visible/physical representations or images of the invisible God, and who are made as creations distinct from God; of the complete goodness of the material creation; of the space-time fall that brings evil into every aspect of human experience.

These ideas of Plotinus came into the Christian church both in the West and in the East—even more strongly in the East through Dionysius the Areopagite. Dionysius's name comes from the Dionysius mentioned in Acts 17 as being converted through the ministry of Paul in Athens. It was later realized, however, that he lived in the fifth century A.D. The mystical theology in parts of the Eastern Orthodox Church is deeply influenced by these Neoplatonic teachings that come from pseudo-Dionysius. Vladimir Lossky expresses the significance of mysticism for the Eastern Orthodox church in this way: "Mysticism is . . . the perfecting and crown of all theology . . . theology *par excellence*."[6]

This elevated view of mysticism leads to the following emphases:

- In this mystical tradition, the end of mysticism is to transcend all knowledge; the ultimate end is union with God, or "deification."
- The whole purpose of the Christian life and of all the struggles of theology through the ages is seen as moving toward and realizing this mystical union with God.
- Christ's purpose in coming was to attain this mystical union with God, or deification, for us.
- Consequently, the monastic life, a life devoted to union with God, is regarded as the most classical form of the spiritual life, for union with God requires a complete renunciation of the life of this present world.

Dionysius the Areopagite
Dionysius wrote of two theological ways:

1. The Cataphatic way: this is the way of positive theology in which the theologian moves ahead by

making affirmations about God—this gives some knowledge of God.

2. The Apophatic way: this is the way of negative theology in which the theologian moves ahead by making negations—this leads to a higher knowledge of God.

This theology teaches that God is unknowable, that he is beyond all that exists, so it encourages the way of total ignorance. Vladimir Lossky, who is clearly a passionate advocate for the mystical way, says that such an approach is the "fundamental characteristic of the whole theological tradition of the Eastern Church."[7]

The purpose of this theology is union with God, a union that is beyond subjectivity ("I perceive God") and beyond objectivity ("God perceives me").

We need to think carefully about what the "way of negation" teaches because this helps us to see some of the problems, from a biblical perspective, of this kind of teaching.

The Way of Negation
What is involved in pursuing this way of negation?

1. Renunciation of the world: This is the nature of true conversion. What is meant by this is not simply turning from one's own way to obey God, but rather turning from "exteriorization," for all exteriorization is sin. The soul is by nature not subject to engagement with the external world, so the aim of renunciation is to no longer be engaged with the world around me. (We need to ask whether this is what Scripture means by "Set your mind on things that are above, not on things that are on the earth" [Col. 3:2], or "friendship with the world is enmity

with God" [James 4:4], or "Do not love the world or the things in the world" [1 John 2:15].)

2. Impassibility: The goal of the spiritual life is to attain a state wherein one is not affected by anything; wherein one is neither passive nor active; wherein one experiences neither pleasure nor pain, but is simply vigilant. (Is this what it means for us to "wait for the LORD" [Isa. 40:31]?) We also need to ask whether this impassibility is ever encouraged by Scripture. Is this what Paul means when he writes to the Philippians of learning the secret of being content, whether he has plenty or little, whether he is abased or whether he abounds? Can we square this approach with 1 John 4:20's teaching: how can we say we love God whom we have not seen if we do not love man whom we do see? What are we to say to the many other passages of Scripture that encourage us to take delight in our life here in this world, or to weep with those who weep and to rejoice with those who rejoice? Such texts seem to express approval of our personal and deeply emotional engagement in the human world.

3. Prayer: Active prayer in which we use words to speak to God is just beginning prayer. This should lead us on to passionlessness, for this is the frontier of prayer. Wordless prayer, contemplative prayer, in which the soul lays itself bare in silence before God is true prayer. This approach to prayer leads us to "the end of petition." (Again, we need to ask whether this end of petition is what the Scriptures teach us about prayer; or whether our being encouraged to wait on the Lord or to be silent before the Lord is Scripture encouraging wordless contemplative prayer of the passionless kind that the mystics envisage.)

4. Repentance: Here "repentance" is understood to mean not so much a turning away from sin, but rather a

"continuous exodus from oneself." (We need to ask what the Scripture means by its call to crucify ourselves, to deny ourselves, and to die with Christ. We also need to ask whether the Scripture does indeed demand that we ourselves die and "stay dead," as Watchman Nee teaches. If this view is correct, then we must believe that the mind, emotions, and will must constantly be put to death—again, this is what Watchman Nee teaches, and it is an understanding that has deeply affected evangelical spirituality, as well as the mystical tradition. Is it not rather the case that Scripture clearly teaches that we not only die with Christ, but are also raised with Christ? As those raised with Christ, we are now living by faith in him. Our spiritual calling is that we ourselves—our emotions, our minds, our wills, our whole being, including ultimately our bodies—are to be renewed so that we become human persons who are like God.)

This reflection, and the questions asked about the way of negation and its disagreement with Scripture, brings us to look more carefully at some of the central theological emphases in the mystical tradition.

THEOLOGICAL EMPHASES OF THE MYSTICAL TRADITION

The nine theological emphases that follow are found both within elements of Eastern Orthodoxy and within parts of the Western church. I do not want to suggest that the whole of either the Eastern church or the Western church has been shaped by the mystical tradition from Dionysius. Eastern Orthodox theologians, such as Vladimir Lossky, may insist that the mystical tradition is the dominant, and finest, understanding of Eastern Orthodoxy. Many Orthodox Christians, however, will not recognize themselves and their understanding of their Christian faith either in his passionate defense of mysticism or in the summary below of theological emphases in the mystical tradition. This will be especially true for those members of Orthodox churches who have come from an evangelical Protestant background and whose feet are very firmly planted in biblical theology and in a biblical worldview. This is also true of large sections of the Orthodox Church here in the United States, for Orthodox theology here has been far more influenced by both Western and Protestant theology and practice than is true in much of the Orthodox Church in Greece or in Russia (in both many might also question mysticism's centrality).

1. The Oneness of God tends to be emphasized over against the triune nature of God. I am not suggesting that the doctrine of the Trinity disappears, for as long as anyone in the mystical theological tradition keeps one foot in Scripture, the acknowledgment of Father, Son, and Spirit as three persons will continue. But the point stands: the more strong the move toward mysticism, the less emphasis on the Trinity and the more emphasis on the Oneness of God. My qualifications in this first point also apply to each of the following points. The more fully the mystical tradition is embraced, especially the way of negation, the more the person will move in the direction of each emphasis named. The more the person is anchored in Scripture, the less he or she will move in the direction of each emphasis.

2. There tends to be an obscuring, or downplaying, of the personal nature of God. This is an inevitable consequence of the way of negation. If we think the way of

negation is indeed a higher way, then we must agree that this approach does give us a truer, or deeper, knowledge of God. If we pursue the goal of the negative way, and then take away all the things we can say about God, the following consequence must follow. Take this example: "I affirm that God is the three persons of the Trinity who have loved each other and communicated with each other through all eternity." If I then take the negative way, I have to say that such a statement about God does not help me to understand God better; it gets me no closer to describing who he is. The implication of the negative way is that God is beyond naming and that we can meet him in his true essence only through removing affirmations about him, including the affirmations about eternal love between the members of the Trinity. We need to compare this approach to the wonderful words of Jesus in his High Priestly Prayer to the Father in John chapter 17. There we see the eternal Son delighting in his personal relationship of love with the Father, a love that existed before the universe was made. This is the deepest knowledge we can have of God. We need to proceed not by negations, but rather by these glorious affirmations.

3. We will tend to find an emphasis on the spiritual nature of man as the area of our uniqueness rather than the image of God. Scripture, in contrast, declares that we are made as physical, visible, finite representations of the invisible, infinite God.

4. The incarnation of Christ becomes central, for it is the means of deifying man, rather than the substitutionary atonement at the heart of the gospel being the means of dealing with the moral problem of our sin.

5. The "in Christ" language of the New Testament is understood as mystical union rather than representation,

headship, justification, or substitution. Deification, or "enwsis," union with God, is the consequence of Christ's work for us in this tradition.

6. There is an equating of sin with "being a self," a particular person. So our problem tends to become an ontological one: we are created beings; we are selves, with a particular existence; and this existing as self-conscious selves becomes our problem. The Scripture insists, in contrast, that our problem is not ontological, but moral: we are persons who have rebelled against God, we have broken his laws, and we face his moral and just judgment.

7. There is devaluation of the mind and of rational understanding, for this is considered inferior to direct apprehension of God.

8. There is devaluation of language and of doctrine; all language is ultimately idolatrous. This leads to the devaluation of Scripture, both because Scripture is "merely language" and because words about God are regarded as inferior to the direct experience of God, which then tends to become the ultimate spiritual authority.

9. This tradition tends to emphasize techniques for practicing the presence of God: means for emptying the self; repetitive prayer to engage the surface mind and quiet the soul; states of vigilance that will prepare the soul to be a vessel ready for union with God.

As we consider these emphases or directions of the mystical tradition, one observation that necessarily arises is this: one can find these emphases and these spiritual leanings in mystics from very different religious traditions, both Christian and non-Christian. This reality should encourage the Christian to pause before too readily embracing mysticism.

Unity of Mystics from All Traditions

Let's go back to our first definition of "mysticism" from two of the best known recent commentators on this approach to spirituality:

> The belief that the human spirit, finite, limited and clouded though it is, can nevertheless experience the presence of the Divine Reality which undergirds and permeates the world.[8]

> Mysticism, in its pure form, is the science of ultimates, the science of union with the Absolute, and nothing else, and . . . the mystic is the person who attains this union. . . . The end which the mystic sets before him is conscious union with a living Absolute.[9]

One does not need to have a critical spirit or to be a cynic to observe that these definitions sound suspiciously akin to pantheism. Recognizing this, some Christian defenders of the mystical way of understanding the Christian life will try to ameliorate the pantheistic implications of a metaphysical union with Deity. They do this by insisting that Catholic and Orthodox theologians, even when they speak of the soul's absorption into God, declare that the soul retains its own individuality and full personality. The intent of such statements is to try to defend the mystics' goal, methods, and experience as legitimately Christian. But when you read the mystics themselves, as Georgia Harkness herself acknowledges, they slide often into an "ontological merging of the finite with the Infinite for a transient but ecstatic period. This . . . goes back to Plotinus and Neo-Platonism as it was introduced into Christianity through Augustine, hovers on the borderline of pantheism while endeavoring to retain belief in the personal God of biblical Christian faith."[10]

William James, one of the primary scholars researching mystical and other religious states in an earlier generation, wrote the classic study *Varieties of Religious Experience.* He commented that even though some theologians may protest about his conclusions, if the mystic teaches us that we cannot express in words the truth about God, then doctrine is essentially unimportant. He writes of mystical states: "This overcoming of all the usual barriers between the individual and the Absolute is the great mystic achievement. In mystic states we both become one with the Absolute and aware of our oneness. This is the everlasting and triumphant mystical tradition, hardly altered by differences of clime or creed. In Hinduism, in Neoplatonism, in Sufism, in Christian mysticism, in Whitmanism, we find the same recurring note, so that there is about mystical utterances an eternal unanimity which ought to make a critic stop and think, and which brings it about that the mystical classics have, as has been said, neither birthday nor native land. Perpetually telling of the unity of man with God, their speech antedates languages, and they do not grow old."[11]

After his discussion of prayer James summarizes his conclusions in this way: "I said awhile ago that the religious attitude of Protestants appears poverty-stricken to the Catholic imagination."[12] It is evident that this is James's own view, for he writes, again comparing Catholic and Protestant approaches to the religious imagination: "How flat does evangelical Protestantism appear, how bare the atmosphere of those isolated religious lives whose boast it is that 'man in the bush with God may meet.' What a pulverization and leveling of what a gloriously piled-up structure. To an imagination used to the perspectives of dignity and glory, the naked gospel scheme seems to offer an almshouse for a palace."[13] James seems puzzled by evangelical Christians who abandon the search for mystical experience, and he writes with considerable derision about petitionary prayer, holding up George Mueller as a particularly ridiculous example. James writes: "Muller's prayers were of the crassest petitional order" and he refers to "the extraordinary narrowness of the man's intellectual horizon."[14]

All through this essay I have raised questions about the mystical tradition, questions that point to areas in which the mystics begin to move away from the teaching and practice found in the Scriptures. In this next section, some of the additional basic questions that need to be asked are set out in a more formal way.

Some Questions to Ask about Mysticism

1. Is the inner world higher than the outer world? Is the world of spirit within higher than the world of the visible, the material, the world of the senses, of the mind, and of knowledge?
2. Is the Creator/creature distinction ever truly obscured in Scripture?
3. Does true spirituality have to do with withdrawal from the world and from normal social and personal relationships?
4. Is the knowledge of God ever spoken of by Scripture as beyond the awareness of subject and object?
5. Is it biblical to regard all language about God as essentially idolatrous?

These questions (and the ones asked earlier in this essay) lead us to our final section: a restatement of some essential biblical teachings that move the believer away from mysticism.

Biblical Emphases That Militate Against Mysticism

1. In Scripture God presents himself as truly personal, as the three persons of the Father, the Son, and the Holy Spirit. God's personal nature is at the center of who God is. This way of speaking about God is not condescension to use language that will be understandable to us. For example, when Jesus teaches us to pray, "Our Father in heaven" (Matt. 6:9), we are not giving a name to someone who cannot be named. The notion of fatherhood truly expresses God's relationship to us. We cannot penetrate God's essential being more deeply than the way he is revealed to us in Jesus' prayer to the Father on the night before he died, the High Priestly Prayer recorded for us in John chapter 17. In that prayer Jesus speaks of the love and the glory he has shared with the Father from before the creation of the universe. The truth is that our fundamental nature as personal beings becomes meaningful and understandable because it is rooted in the personal nature of God. He is the Father from whom every family in heaven and on earth derives its name. Because he is truly personal, we can speak of our being personal. Because he is love, we can speak of our being made for love. Because the members of the Trinity have an eternal relationship, we can speak of the true beauty of human relationships. We are not naming God from our human experience. It is the other way around: we are naming human experience from our knowledge of God—from who God is in himself.

2. There is a true value to the external and material world—this physical universe—because it is God's good creation. This world is not here simply to serve as a catalyst, the means of setting off a spark to ignite mystical experience. Rather, God has declared it good. The world was good when

he made it. The world is good now (despite Satan's usurping claim to be its ruler). The world will be good when Christ comes and renews it as the new heaven and new earth. We will live in an external and material world forever, for God made us for just such a life.

3. We have also been designed to be physical and to delight in the goodness of a physical life. Death causes a terrible disruption of this physicality when spirit and body are temporarily torn apart and our bodies decay. But Christ was raised from the dead with a glorious and incorruptible body. That is our destiny also, for we, too, will be raised with immortal bodies. To be human is to be embodied forever, for as Paul says, we do not wish to be "unclothed, but . . . further clothed, so that what is mortal may be swallowed up by life" (2 Cor. 5:4). In the meantime, we must hold to Paul's passionate critique of any form of asceticism (see his words in 1 Timothy 4:1–5).

4. Our basic human problem is not a problem of being, of ontology, of metaphysics, but a moral one. The dilemma of our existence does not consist in our finiteness, or our being persons, or our experience of being a self, or our being physical, or our experience of the distinction between ourselves and the world around us. Rather, our dilemma is our rebellion against God, our idolatry of self, our pride in ourselves, rather than our worship of him. There is no problem with being human, with being finite, with being a person, with being physical, with existing in an external world. The only problem is sin.

5. Understanding the true nature of our human problem helps us to see that the cross is central in the work of Christ as the means of bringing about our justification and redemption. Our problems of sin, the devil, and death must be overcome, and that is what Christ came to do. I

am not intending to devalue the incarnation—the infinite God's being born as a human baby is a mystery that is, of course, beyond our grasp. We worship and adore the loving God who would come down to us in this amazing way. The gospel records teach us, however, that the incarnation looks toward the cross. Christ becomes incarnate so that he might be our representative. He did not become incarnate in order that he might deify human nature, nor that he might take us up back into the Godhead from which we have somehow, by creation, been cut loose. Christ became incarnate to deal with the problem of our sin, of our rebellion, and of the terrible reality of the just judgment that awaits us. Christ's life of righteousness is accounted to us in place of our life of sin. Christ died to be the substitute for us as sinners. Christ's victory on the cross defeats our enemy the devil, who claims us as his subjects because of our sin. Christ's resurrection is his triumph over the death that comes to us because of our sin. Christ's return will be to consummate this victory, so that we might live without sin in his presence forever.

6. Salvation is restoration to a perfect relationship between the Creator and his human creatures. Salvation is also restoration to full reflection of God's character, for we are those who have been made in his likeness and for everlasting fellowship with our Creator. Salvation is not the overcoming of being a self, nor is it being caught up into God. That work of restoration begins at our justification; it continues now as we are being sanctified; and our sanctification will be made complete at death, when our spirits will be made perfect and we go into the presence of the Lord. Then at the coming of Christ our bodies will be raised new, and we will rejoice in eternal and unbroken fellowship with the Father, with the Son, and with the Spirit.

7. At death, and at the coming of Christ, the veil of judgment that hides God from us will be taken away. Now we see in part; then we will know fully as we are now fully known. Then we will see face to face, whereas now we merely see through a glass darkly. We cannot break this glass, nor can we devise means of prayer or meditation that will grant us either brief ecstatic moments of realizing union with God or a steadier state of experiencing his presence. The Scriptures never encourage us to believe that we can engineer this experience of God's presence, or even that we should attempt to do so. We cannot take away the veil that hangs between the seen and unseen world, though of course we long to take it away, for it is certainly true that the veil is a sorrow, a tragedy that we must endure as part of the penalty for our sin. At death the veil will be taken away, and that is why Paul says that it is far better to die and to be with the Lord. Until then it is God's prerogative to pull back this veil at moments of his choosing. And while we may ask him to do this for us, any answer to this kind of prayer is of his sovereign choosing. No means are available to us that will either ensure that such moments will happen or even appropriately prepare us for the possibility that God will grant the experience of the veil's being removed. While we may understand the mystic's desire to see through the veil or to set the veil aside, if the mystic suggests that particular prayers or practices will produce the realization of God's presence, then we must conclude that the mystic's approach is an attempt to "force God's hand." But we cannot force his hand in this or in any other way.

8. We should also conclude that we are not to devalue the mind and rational knowledge, for this is how God has created us to know. No way of negation is encouraged by the Scriptures, but rather, only the way of affirmation. This

is not to say that our knowledge is only rational, for it is also relational, volitional, imaginative, emotional, and physical, since this, too, is how God has made us to be. In addition, this is not to say that our knowledge is ever exhaustive, for because of our finiteness our knowledge will always be limited and incomplete. Because God is so far above us, it is clear that we will never know him fully. This will still be true ten thousand years after Christ comes to establish his kingdom. We will still be overwhelmed by the transcendent glory and majesty of God. There will still be inexhaustible riches of his might and power, his love and grace, his being and character, to discover and never fully penetrate. So it will be forever. Knowledge, however, when it is in accord with God's revelation of himself, can be faithful. We can indeed have true knowledge of God himself.

9. Language is the appropriate way to express our knowledge of God and to make our thanks, praise, and desires known to him. The reason for this is that language is so fundamental to our being made in God's likeness that it must not be devalued. Again, this is not to say that words can completely capture our knowledge of God, nor that words can express all that we long to communicate to God, for we all have groanings too deep for words. This is true in our relationships with one another as well. Love in marriage, love in family, love in friendship—love is always far more than words can express. And this is true even of our response to the beauties of creation. This is why we delight in the gifts of music and painting and sculpture as well as in verbal accounts of our response to the wonders of life. But again, to acknowledge that there can be more than words can express in our relationship with God, with one another, and with the world is not to deny or to denigrate the value of language. Christ himself is the eternal Word.

Communication in language is at the heart of the nature of God, and communication in language is fundamental to our existence as those made in his image.

10. Biblical meditation is rich in content. In Scripture, meditation is never presented as a way of emptying the mind and heart of true understanding of God and of his Word, nor is meditation ever presented as a way of emptying the mind of appropriate response to the Lord and to his revelation to us. Meditation is to be on God's works (Ps. 77:12; 119:27; 143:5; 145:5). It is to be on God's promises (Ps. 119:48). It is to be on God's Word (Col. 3:16). It is to be on his laws (Josh. 1:8; Ps. 1:2; 119:15, 48, 97, 99). It is to be on his love (Ps. 48:9). Meditation is thinking about God, remembering him all night long (Ps. 63:6); it is gazing on the beauty of the Lord (Ps. 27:4). Meditation is storing up the Word in my heart so that I might not sin against God (Ps. 119:11); meditation is having a heart that is so full of a desire to please and obey God that my thoughts are acceptable to him (Ps. 19:14; 104:34).

11. For this present time we must learn to be content to walk by faith and not by sight—even though we may groan because we are burdened down with sin and the troubles that come into our lives. Because of this sad reality of our broken lives now, and the tragedy of the veil between us and God, we may, quite rightly, long to be clothed with our heavenly dwelling. Of course we are eager for the Lord to come. We know that it would be far better to be with him. But he calls us to be of good courage, living in the hope of the future realization of the full presence of God in our experience and the complete realization of all his promises to us. Then we will realize how brief and transient this present difficult time is, for we are being prepared for an eternal weight of glory beyond all comparison.

Appendix B

The "Extra Words" of the Lord's Prayer

A question is frequently asked about the "extra words" that appear with the Lord's Prayer in some translations of the form of the prayer found in Matthew's gospel:

> For yours is the kingdom and the power and the glory, forever. Amen. (Matt. 6:13)

From where do these extra words come? Or, perhaps, where have they gone? The reader who has an NIV or an ESV will probably find these words included in footnotes. In the King James Bible, these words are part of the text. Why is this line present in some versions of the Bible and not in others?

The answer to this question has to do with different manuscripts of the gospels. The extra words appear in some early manuscripts of Matthew's gospel, and they appear in those manuscripts that were available at the time the KJV translation was made into English (the early 1600s). In the past two hundred years, however, many more manuscripts of the New Testament text have been discovered, and these extra words are not in the very earliest and most reliable of the manuscripts we have. It is probably appropriate, therefore, to conclude that these words were not part of the prayer when Jesus first taught it to his disciples. This is why most recent translations put the extra words in the footnotes rather than in the text.

But the extra words do appear in some early manuscripts. They also appear in another book from the early church, a writing called the "Didache" (or "Teaching of the Apostles"). This text probably comes from the first decades of the second century. Its origin may be even earlier.

The early provenance of the extra words may well mean that they go back to the time of the apostles. One possible explanation is that these words were a congregational response to the one leading the Lord's Prayer, a response made after the Lord's Prayer had been prayed in public worship.

It is also possible that the extra words were taught by Jesus to his disciples on another occasion. If we compare the two versions that we have, the one in Matthew chapter 6 and the other in Luke chapter 11, we know that Jesus taught the prayer in slightly different forms on the two occasions described for us. He may have taught the Lord's Prayer at other times as well. It is also possible that the extra words were used by Jesus himself in his own prayers, and that they were overheard by one of the disciples and then written down.

It is probably right, however, to recognize that these words were not part of the original teaching by Jesus in the Sermon on the Mount setting of Matthew chapter 6. The manuscript evidence is quite clear.

One additional point needs to be made. The extra words themselves are thoroughly biblical in their meaning and expression. A great many passages of Scripture echo the same thoughts as the extra words: "For yours is the kingdom and the power and the glory, forever. Amen."

I mention this last point so that we all may know that it is not wrong in any way to pray the extra words, even if we conclude that there is no clear proof that they were taught by Jesus. Christians have been praying these extra words for almost two thousand years. We can be sure that they please the Lord, for they express the truth.

Appendix C

POSTURE IN PRAYER

W henever I teach on prayer, people come to me afterward and ask questions about the issue of posture in prayer. How are we to think about this?

The simplest place to begin answering this question is to look at the information we have about Jesus. We will look at the accounts of Jesus praying in the garden of Gethsemane, just before his betrayal by Judas and his subsequent arrest. The gospel writers describe what happened in this way:

> And going a little farther he fell on his face and prayed . . . . (Matt. 26:39)

> And going a little farther, he fell on the ground and prayed . . . . (Mark 14:35)

> He withdrew from them about a stone's throw, and knelt down and prayed . . . . (Luke 22:41)

If we try to put these three descriptions together, we may perhaps assume that Jesus knelt at first and then prostrated himself on the ground as his distress and prayers became more intense. We can say this with certainty: his extreme sorrow is expressed physically. We may assume, without any likelihood of misrepresenting the truth, that this was not the only occasion in Jesus' life that he knelt or that he lay facedown to pray, for what Jesus does in Gethsemane reflects commonly used biblical language and frequently described practice.

For example, Luke gives us a very moving description of the time of prayer and then the parting between Paul and the people after his account of Paul's meeting with the elders and with others from the churches in Ephesus:

> And when he had said these things, he knelt down and prayed with them all. And there was much weeping on the part of all; they embraced Paul and kissed him, being sorrowful most of all because of the word he had spoken, that they would not see his face again. (Acts 20:36–38a)

In his first letter to Timothy, Paul writes about "lifting holy hands" in prayer (1 Tim. 2:8), and he describes his own prayers by referring to the physical posture that accompanies them: "I bow my knees before the Father" (Eph. 3:14). We should assume, I think, not that this is simply a figure of speech, but rather that these words give an accurate physical description of the way in which Paul prayed. Both in public and in private, Paul's practice was to kneel—perhaps not on every occasion, but often.

If we turn to the Old Testament, we find many passages that teach us a similar approach toward physical expression in worship and prayer. The terms "bow down" and "bow the knee" are synonyms for worship (see, e.g., Ex. 20:5; Deut. 5:9; Isa. 45:23). This latter passage is repeated in the New Testament in Paul's hymn to Christ (Phil. 2:10; see also Dan. 3:4–7, 11; Rom. 11:4; 14:11).

We repeatedly find the following kind of language when the psalmist calls on the people of God to worship:

> Oh come, let us worship and bow down;
>   Let us kneel before the LORD, our Maker! (Ps. 95:6)

We find examples of the people of God obeying this injunction and kneeling to pray and worship (Dan. 6:10; see also v. 5). We find other examples of believers' prostrating themselves in prayer (Deut. 9:18; Ps. 38:6; Isa. 49:7) and of believers' bowing their heads in prayer (Ps. 35:13–14). We also see people clapping their hands (Ps. 47:1), raising their hands (Ps. 134:2), and dancing before the Lord (Ps. 149:3; 150:4; see also the examples of Miriam and David in Ex. 15:20 and 2 Sam. 6:14).

We may conclude from these biblical examples that physical expression accompanying worship is the biblical norm. Physical expression is not something exceptional or excessive.

This uniform biblical teaching of the appropriateness and naturalness of physical expression accompanying prayer and worship raises a challenge for us. We may express this challenge in the form of two questions: "Why do many of us, both in our private devotion and in public worship in our churches, feel uncomfortable with kneeling to pray or with lying prostrate in prayer; with raising our hands in intercession, in praise, or in blessing; with clapping our hands in praise; or even with dancing in the worship of the Lord?" "Why are we uncomfortable with and even suspicious of such practices, when they are clearly biblical?"

There are several reasons for the discomfort. Some are historical; some are cultural. One of the reasons is that some of us have been raised up in churches where physical expression is frowned on as an excessive and attention-getting display, even as somehow unspiritual and carnal.

In some of our church traditions, this view that physical expression is carnal is a reaction to the dramatic visual and physical ritual of the medieval church, and so kneeling, lying prostrate, and raising hands are seen as somehow spiritually dangerous. In the same manner and for the same reasons, some of our traditions are suspicious of religious art, of ornamentation in church buildings, of robes for the pastor, or of decorated cloths on the communion table.

We may look back at the sixteenth century and have understanding and sympathy for the reactions to medieval practice that took place during the Reformation. Yet the Reformation happened nearly five hundred years ago, and we ought not to be governed by all the reactions of our traditions, no matter how much we treasure them in essential matters of doctrine and practice. John Calvin himself said that tradition is a good guide, but a poor master. Our Master is, in all things, the Lord speaking through his Word in the Scriptures. We must move beyond reaction and tradition to a faithful biblical emphasis on the proper place of the physical in prayer and worship.

Sometimes the negative views of physical expression arise from the idea that true spirituality is as bare, unphysical, and unartistic as possible. Some churches have held this approach with passionate consistency, even devaluing the Lord's Supper and baptism. In some traditions, the sacraments are regarded as unnecessary physical portrayals of God's commitment to us. They are God's condescension to our weakness and for those with little faith. But for those who have a deep understanding and a deep appreciation of the spiritual nature of God and of true worship, such physical expressions are no longer necessary.

While most would not take this extreme a view, there is still a deep suspicion of physical expression in much of the Protestant church. This suspicion assumes that the nature of Old Testament worship—with its beautiful temple and rich interior decoration, its glorious music and choirs of singers, its priests arrayed in robes and jewels, its incense and ritual, its clapping, raising hands, and dancing—reflected a stage of spiritual infancy or immaturity. Such visual and sensual display was for the time of promise and preparation only. Now that Christ has come to fulfill all that Old Testament worship pictured, the time of infancy, immaturity, and preparation is over. The people of God are to put the childish away, and we are to develop a more spiritual, and therefore a less physical and less aesthetic, worship experience.

The problems with such a view are many. The most obvious problem is this: God himself mandated the tabernacle and temple worship for his people, not Moses or Solomon. In addition, the Scripture makes it clear that the pattern of the temple and of its worship is found in heaven, not in some place of spiritual infancy. Old Testament worship is a copy of the heavenly original.

This observation leads us to another: the same kind of physical and aesthetic worship that we see in the Old Testament reappears in John's vision of heavenly worship (see Revelation chapters 4 and 5). The elders gathered around God's throne can hardly be accused of being unspiritual and immature when they prostrate themselves before the Lord!

In addition, we find the same kind of worship in the future kingdom when the new earth and heaven are realized.

The worship of the coming kingdom will be physical and aesthetically glorious. Our future worship will involve our whole being, all that it means to be human, when we assemble in the New Jerusalem to honor and serve the King of kings.

In addition to the foregoing problems of discounting the physical and the aesthetic in worship, a profound theological error lurks at the heart of such views. At the center of this suspicion of physical expression in worship and prayer is a deeply unbiblical devaluation of the body, with a corresponding elevation of an imagined purely spiritual life, as if such a life were a superior state. God's Word rejects such a view with great passion. The Lord is delighted that we are physical, and he loves the material and aesthetic nature of our world. Several foundational doctrines make this point clear.

CREATION

See Genesis chapter 1 with God's repeated "it was good," "it was good," "it was good," "it was good," "it was good," "it was very good." The apostle Paul refers back to these words of Genesis when he responds to teaching that devalues physical life and its joys.

Paul's words are perhaps the strongest condemnation of any false doctrine that can be found in Scripture. The reason for this is that any diminishing of the value of our material creation is a kind of blasphemy against God, who made our world physical and beautiful and who made us physical representations of himself.

Now the Spirit expressly says that in later times some will depart from the faith by devoting themselves to deceitful spirits and teachings of demons, through the insincerity of liars whose consciences are seared, who forbid marriage and require abstinence from foods that God created to be received with thanksgiving by those who believe and know the truth. For everything created by God is good, and nothing is to be rejected if it is received with thanksgiving, for it is made holy by the word of God and prayer. (1 Tim. 4:1–5)

COMMON GRACE, OR GOD'S PROVIDENTIAL CARE FOR ALL CREATION

God made an everlasting covenant with all creatures after the flood (Gen. 9:8–17). God cares for *all* creation, and this is celebrated in the Psalms (see, in particular Pss. 104, 145). Jesus also speaks of this in the Sermon on the Mount, when he encourages his disciples by describing our heavenly Father as watching over and providing for the flowers and the birds, and even more for all people (Matt. 6:26–29; 10:29–31).

THE INCARNATION

The eternal Son of God, the second person of the Trinity, became flesh; he became a man; he became a part of our physical universe. Our Lord became physical not only for the thirty-three years of his earthly life, but for all eternity to come. That is why we will see him face to face and rejoice in his glorious presence. That is why we will be served by him at his table in the kingdom to come. That is why we will eat with him and drink the fruit of the vine with him at the marriage supper of the Lamb (see Matt. 26:29; Luke 12:37; Rev. 2:7; 19:9; and many other passages that describe our seeing Christ and being physically in his presence).

BODILY RESURRECTION

Paul writes joyful words about our physical resurrection (1 Cor. 15; 2 Cor. 5:1–5). Nothing expresses with greater clarity that our physical life in this world is precious than our conviction that God is committed "not that we would be unclothed, but that we would be further clothed, so that what is mortal may be swallowed up by life" (2 Cor. 5:4).

THE NEW CREATION

There will be a renewed earth, with the curse removed (see Rom. 8:18–25; 2 Peter 3:13; Rev. 21:1–4). This promise of the glory of the earth to come underlines the significance and value of all that God has made for our enjoyment here and now: things to entrance our eyes and ravish all our senses. Our redemption will not be complete until our human life is restored to its full delight in the wonder of God's good and beautiful creation.

The Lord has made us as physical/spiritual beings. This is who we are, and it is good. God has never regretted that he made us physical, or that both he and we take joy in beauty. This is our nature forever. In the kingdom to come, we will be raised up with immortal and incorruptible bodies. This will make us glad. We will have no shame about our bodies. We will not worry about what others may think of us for being too emotional or too physically expressive. Indeed, we might ask, is it possible to be too emotional or too expressive about Christ dying for us?

To these foundational doctrines that affirm the value of the body, we may add a brief word about the nature of the sacraments. God has given us physical signs and seals of his love for us in baptism and the Lord's Supper. These visible and physical signs and seals are not concessions to our weakness, but rather gifts that are appropriate for our physical nature. We are embodied beings. That is not something unfortunate; it is who we are intended to be. The signs and seals of baptism and the Lord's Supper are physical promises, visible and tangible words showing us the love of Christ.

These signs and seals are found in every stage of the life of the kingdom of God, from creation all the way through to consummation: the Tree of Life in the garden; the sacrifices after the fall; the rainbow; circumcision; the Passover; the ceremony of the ratification of the covenant (Ex. 24); the sacrificial system; baptism and the Lord's Supper; and the marriage supper of the Lamb and the Tree of Life in the kingdom to come.

One more point needs to be made. In our human relationships, physical expression is natural to us. We embrace; we kiss; we clap; we raise our hands; we fall on our knees; we lie prostrate. We do these things spontaneously, whenever these responses and actions are appropriate. So it should be in our relationship with the Lord, for we are called to honor him with our bodies (Rom. 12:1; 1 Cor. 6:20).

It is simply not biblical to say that the less emotional, the less expressive, the less ornamented, the less imaginative, and the less beautiful, the more spiritual worship is. In the life to come, we will know that such a view is completely nonsensical. We should start getting used to the joyful truth now, the truth that God has designed us to worship him with our whole being, and so prepare ourselves for the coming kingdom.

NOTES

Chapter 3: Two Stories about Prayer

1. Jordan Fisher Smith, *Nature Noir: A Park Ranger's Patrol in the Sierra* (New York: Houghton Mifflin Company, 2005), 9–10.

Chapter 10: Jesus Prays for Glory

1. John Calvin, *Commentary on the Gospel According to John* (Calvin Translation Society; repr., Grand Rapids: Baker Book House, 1984), 2:164.

Chapter 11: Jesus Prays for His People

1. John Calvin, *Commentaries on the Last Four Books of Moses Arranged in the Form of a Harmony* (Calvin Translation Society; repr., Grand Rapids: Baker Book House, 1984), 3:10. Calvin is commenting on the promise of the fifth commandment, and he adds these words: "Here the question arises, since this earthly life is exposed to so many cares, and pains, and troubles, how can God account its prolongation to be a blessing?"

Chapter 12: Jesus Prays for Unity

1. Robert N. Bellah, et al., *Habits of the Heart: Individualism and Commitment in American Life* (Berkeley, CA: University of California Press, 1985, 1996, 2007).

2. Jerram Barrs, *The Heart of Evangelism* (Wheaton, IL: Crossway Books, 2001), 121–23.

Appendix A: An Essay on Mysticism and Prayer

1. Georgia Harkness, *Mysticism: Its Meaning and Message* (London: Oliphants, 1973), 18.

2. Evelyn Underhill, *Mysticism* (London: Methuen & Co. Ltd., 17th ed., 1949). Underhill makes this point many times. On page 4: "the object of man's craving; the only satisfying goal of his quest" is "establishing immediate communication between the spirit of man . . . and that 'only Reality,' that immaterial and final Being, which some philosophers call the Absolute, and most theologians call God." On page 72: "Mysticism, in its pure form, is the science of ultimates, the science of union with the Absolute, and nothing else, and that the mystic is the person who attains this union." On page 73: ". . . the end which the mystic sets before him is conscious union with a living Absolute."

3. Harkness, *Mysticism: Its Meaning and Message*, 36–37.

4. These words are found in B. B. Warfield's wonderful essay "Mysticism and Christianity," in *Studies in Theology*, pages 647–66, vol. 9, *The Works of Benjamin Breckenridge Warfield* (New York: Oxford University Press, 1932; repr., Grand Rapids: Baker Book House, 1981), pages 651–52. This is one of the most helpful discussions of the difference between Christian faith and mysticism that I have been able to discover and is most certainly worth reading in full. The words in the text appear in the following paragraph from Warfield's essay:

"The great variety of the accounts which mystics give of the feeling to which they make their appeal arises from the very nature of the case. There is a deeper reason for a mystic being 'mute'—that is what the name imports—than that he wishes to make a mystery of his discoveries. He is 'mute' because, as a mystic, he has nothing to say. When he sinks within himself he finds feelings, not conceptions; his is an emotional, not a conceptional, religion; and feelings, emotions, though not inaudible, are not articulate. As a mystic, he has no conceptional language in which to express what he feels. If he attempts to describe it he must make use of terms derived from the religious or philosophical thought in vogue about him, that is to say, of non-mystical language. His hands may be the hands of Esau, but his voice is the voice of Jacob. The language in which he describes the reality which he finds within him does not in the least indicate, then, what it is; it is merely a concession to the necessity of communicating with the external world or with his own more external self. What he finds within him is just to his apprehension an 'unutterable abyss.' And Synesius does himself and his fellow mystics no injustice when he declares that 'the mystic mind says this and that, gyrating around the unutterable abyss.' " (Synesius was a bishop a little after the year AD 400 in Ptolemais in Libya. His thinking was deeply influenced by neo-Platonism.)

5. When I was in India visiting the temples of one of Hinduism's most holy places, I noticed that very few Hindu priests were present. During the afternoon of our time there, the priests returned from a month of meditation in the forests above their temples. Inquiring about this, I learned that their month had been spent in fasting, meditation, and mystical experience. It was sobering to see them, for they looked emaciated and unkempt, and some of them seemed literally to be "out of their minds."

6. Vladimir Lossky, *The Mystical Theology of the Eastern Church* (London: James Clarke & Co. Ltd., 1957, 1968), 9.

7. Lossky, *Mystical Theology*, 26.

8. Harkness, *Mysticism: Its Meaning and Message*, 18.

9. Underhill, *Mysticism*, 72–73.

10. Harkness, *Mysticism: Its Meaning and Message*, 22.

11. William James, *The Varieties of Religious Experience*, The New American Library of World Literature (New York, Signet, 1958), 321.

12. Ibid., 380.

13. Ibid., 349.

14. Ibid., 356.